PETS FROM THE POND

Books by Margaret Waring Buck

IN WOODS AND FIELDS

IN YARDS AND GARDENS

IN PONDS AND STREAMS

SMALL PETS FROM WOODS AND FIELDS

ALONG THE SEASHORE

WHERE THEY GO IN WINTER

PETS FROM THE POND

Written and illustrated by

MARGARET WARING BUCK

Nashville   **ABINGDON PRESS**   New York

37343

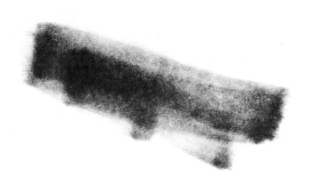

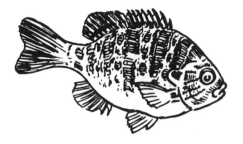

FOR SUSAN

who loves all kinds of pets

This book is for boys and girls who like to catch and keep some of the small creatures that they find in and around ponds and other bodies of water.

It is also for their parents and teachers who are often called upon to help care for the creatures. Simple and practical ways to provide natural homes and acceptable food for water pets are described.

The pets in this book may be found in the northeastern and other parts of the United States and southern Canada.

The author has raised and sketched from life most of the creatures mentioned. In addition, each chapter has been checked by a leading authority on the subject.

The author wishes to express thanks and appreciation to James W. Atz, Associate Curator, New York Aquarium, New York Zoological Society; Alice Gray, Scientific Assistant, and Elizabeth Hellmann, The Museum of Natural History; and Fenner A. Chace, Jr., Curator, Division of Marine Invertebrates, and Joseph P. E. Morrison, Division of Mollusks, Smithsonian Institution.

CONTENTS

PETS FROM THE POND

AQUARIUMS

What pets from the pond are you going to raise? The type of aquarium you need depends on the kind of pond visitors you will have. The proper home will mean healthier pets.

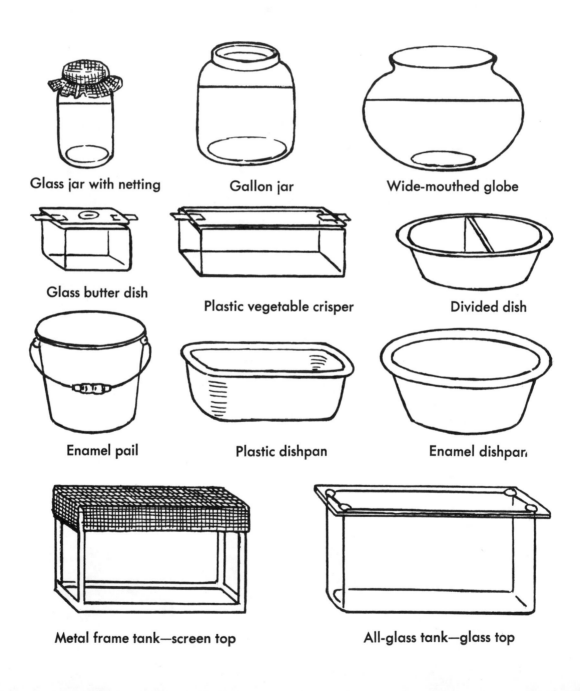

Glass jar with netting

Gallon jar

Wide-mouthed globe

Glass butter dish

Plastic vegetable crisper

Divided dish

Enamel pail

Plastic dishpan

Enamel dishpan

Metal frame tank—screen top

All-glass tank—glass top

Before you go out to look for pets from a pond or other body of water, you must have a container ready for them. Water pets need some kind of an aquarium. You can either buy one from a store, or find something to use for one in your house.

Be sure the aquarium is large enough to give the pets room to move around and oxygen to breathe. It is often better to have a separate container for each kind of pet. Large and small meat-eating pets should not be kept together as the large ones are likely to eat the small ones. Several medium-sized containers are often more practical than one large one.

KITCHEN UTENSIL AQUARIUMS

A container made of glass, plastic, china, or enamel may be used for an aquarium. Do not use a metal container as the metal may make the water poisonous to fishes and other creatures. Some of the containers which may be used are glass jars, butter dishes, refrigerator dishes, casseroles, dishpans, pails, and washtubs. Whatever container is used should have a wide opening to let as much air as possible reach the surface of the water. If a cover is used, leave an air space between it and the container.

AQUARIUMS TO BUY

Gallon jars or globes are inexpensive. They may be used for small pets if they have a wide top opening. A small-mouthed globe if it is more than half full of water, or a tall narrow jar does not let in enough oxygen.

For two or three dollars (or much more for large sizes) you may buy a rectangular tank like the ones at the bottom of page 10. The tank may be all glass, or all plastic, or it may have a metal frame with glass sides and a slate bottom. If you would like to make a rectangular tank, you can buy an aquarium kit containing stainless steel strips for the frame, pieces of glass for the sides and bottom, and aquarium cement from Aljo Aquarium Products, Philadelphia, Pa. The kit costs about the same as a ready-made tank.

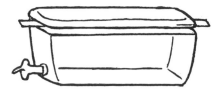

Plastic water cooler

Plastic refrigerator dish

Glass casserole

Enamel basin—glass cover

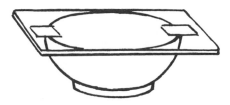

China bowl—glass cover

Enamel washtub

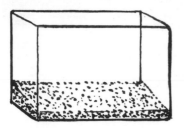

Layer of sand on bottom

Stone and stick above water
for air-breathing creatures

Pouring water
on newspaper

Pouring water into saucer

HOW TO FILL

HOW TO FILL

First make sure the aquarium is clean. See "How to Clean" on page 13. Next check for leaks. Sometimes a tank with a metal frame may have a small leak. If it does, apply aquarium cement to the edges of the glass on the inside. A very small hole may fill up with sand or mud.

Before putting water in the aquarium, spread a layer of sand or fine gravel about two inches deep over the bottom. Have it higher at the back so that dirt will accumulate in front where it may easily be siphoned off. Use bird gravel from a pet store, or sand from a road, yard, or brook; sea sand is too fine. If the sand is dirty, put it in a pail and pour water over it, stir vigorously, then pour the water off. Pebbles, marbles, or coarse gravel are not good to use on the bottom of an aquarium.

When the sand is in place, lay several thicknesses of newspaper over it. Pour water on the paper until the aquarium is ¾ filled. (More water is added after the plants are put in.) The paper prevents the sand from rising and clouding the water. As soon as the water is in, remove the paper.

If water from a pond is used in the aquarium, plant and animal life may be added at once. If house water from a tap is used, it should stand in an open container at least twenty-four hours to allow any chlorine in it to escape. Pouring the water from a spray, such as the nozzle of a watering can, helps to aerate it.

If you are going to keep creatures that breathe air, you should provide something for them to rest on above the water's surface. A few large stones with a flat one on top, a stick anchored in the sand, or a container with earth and plants will serve the purpose.

It is usually better to cover an aquarium to keep dust out and living creatures in. If you use a glass cover, glue thin pieces of cork or cardboard to the top corners of the aquarium and set the glass on them. This makes a small air space. Window screening may be used over some large aquariums. Cut a piece about 2 inches larger than the aquarium on all four sides; cut a square out of each corner and bend the sides down. Mosquito netting or cheesecloth held in place with a rubber band will cover a small opening such as the top of a jar.

HOW TO CLEAN

A new aquarium may be rinsed with clear water and rubbed with a lint-free cloth. A used aquarium is harder to clean because it usually has a brownish or greenish scum on the glass. This can be scraped off with a razor blade in a holder, a rubber scraper, a window cleaner, a copper cleaning pad, a cloth dipped in salt, or steel wool held in a piece of cotton to protect the fingers. If you expect to have snails or tadpoles in the aquarium, some of the green can be left on the glass for them to eat. Do not use soap, detergent, or scouring powder for cleaning.

After your aquarium contains living creatures, droppings will collect on the bottom. The roots of growing plants will absorb some; the rest should be cleaned out. If the bottom of the aquarium is cleaned once a week or oftener and uneaten food removed before its spoils, it will seldom be necessary to change all the water.

Dirt may be siphoned from the bottom with a rubber tube or a dip tube. To use a rubber tube, fill it with water at a sink, hold both ends, and take it to the aquarium. Put one end on the bottom and the other in a pail on the floor. Move the tube over the bottom until all the black stuff has been siphoned off. A short glass tube on the aquarium end of the rubber tube makes it easier to use.

A rubber tube ½ to ¾ of an inch across and 3 to 4 feet long may be purchased at a drugstore. A glass tube 6 to 12 inches long to fit into the rubber tube may be bought at the same place.

A dip tube is bought in an aquarium store. To use it, place the larger end on the bottom of the aquarium while holding your thumb over the small end. Lift your thumb to suck the water up, and turn the tube upside down to empty.

The glass tube from the end of the siphon may be used as a dip tube, but it is a slow process. After the dirty water fills the tube, place your thumb over the top, lift it out, and empty it.

Rescue any snails or other small life that may get sucked up by the tube. Sand may be washed and re-used. The water may be strained through a cloth and returned to the aquarium. Or the aquarium may be refilled with pond water or aerated tap water.

Copper pad

SALT

Steel wool

Razor blade

Rubber scraper

Window cleaner

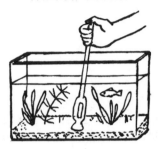

Dip tube

Rubber tube siphon

HOW TO CLEAN

PLANTS

*If you place water plants in your aquarium your water pets
will be healthier and more at home. The plants will make
it like the natural pond or stream that was their home.*

Plants help to make the aquarium attractive; they give off oxygen during the day; and they provide food, shade, shelter, and sometimes a place for water creatures to lay eggs. Most kinds of plants that grow under water may be tried in an aquarium if they are not too large. Select plants with small leaves and small roots or take a few pieces from larger plants.

The small water plants have few flowers or seeds. Some of them form new plants by sending out runners from near the roots; some break off and take root. Never collect more than a few plants at a time. Your aquarium does not need them, but the place where they grow probably does.

WHERE TO FIND AND HOW TO COLLECT

Look along the shallow edges of lakes, ponds, swamps, slow streams, and pools for plants that grow on or under the surface of the water. Look also in wet meadows.

Be prepared to get your feet wet and muddy. Take along something to dig with such as a trowel, digging fork, knife, or shovel. For unexpected digging you can use a forked or pointed stick or a flat stone.

Take some watertight containers for carrying the plants home—a pail, tin cans, milk or cheese cartons. A box or a basket lined with newspapers is useful, too.

To dig the plant up, cut around the roots without disturbing them more than necessary. Plants growing on a stone or other support should be taken with a piece of what they are growing on. Floating plants may be taken without roots; break off a few stems or pull up a handful. Always keep water plants moist.

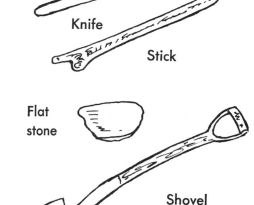

Digging fork   Trowel

Knife

Stick

Flat stone

Shovel

FOR DIGGING

Tin cans

Basket lined with newspapers

Half milk carton

Ice cream or cheese container

Pail

FOR CARRYING

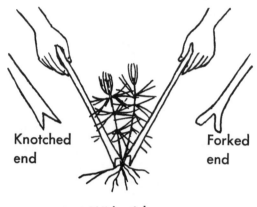

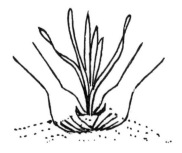

Uprooted stems held
in place by stone

Knotched
end

Forked
end

With sticks

With fork

With fingers

HOW TO PLANT

HOW TO PLANT

If your aquarium has sand in the bottom and has been partly filled with water (as explained on page 12), it is ready for plants.

Before putting the plants into the aquarium, rinse or spray all leaves and stems to remove any harmful insects or parasites that may be on them.

For planting you may use your fingers, a fork, or two sticks. If you use sticks, make a V-shaped notch in the end of each one so that it will hold the plant. Or you may be lucky enough to find two sticks with forked ends that you can use.

Lower the plant into the partly filled aquarium, allow the roots to spread out, then press them into the sand until they are covered. Do not set deeply enough to cover stems or leaves with sand. If the plant seems wobbly, lay one or two small flat stones over the roots. To plant unrooted stems, push the cut ends into the sand in small bunches or one at a time, and anchor with a stone. Set the taller plants at the back of the aquarium and the shortest ones in front. Plants that float on top go in last.

After all the plants are in place, gently pour in enough water to fill the aquarium to within an inch or two of the top. Give the plants a week or so to take root and start to grow before you put any animal life in with them.

WHERE TO KEEP

Plants need to be near a light window or an electric light that is on throughout the day. Some kinds require more sunlight than others. When you collect the plants, notice whether they are growing in a sunny or a shaded place. Most plants will grow in an aquarium placed near a window that gets about two hours of sunlight in the early morning or the late afternoon. Too much sun, especially in summer, will overheat the water. It will also cause a green or brown scum to form on the glass. If you must keep the aquarium in a very sunny window, put a piece of cardboard between it and the window.

On the following pages are some of the water plants that you are likely to find growing out of doors which will do well in an aquarium.

WATER MOSSES

Some kinds of mosses grow on sticks, stones, and logs in ponds and streams. They will also grow in an aquarium. When collecting them, take a piece of what they are growing on.

In many ponds you will see YELLOWISH-BROWN MOSS with thin, branched stems that form a soft mat. Take a little for your tadpoles, catfish, and snails to eat.

In cool, flowing streams two kinds of FOUNTAIN, or WILLOW, MOSSES grow. One kind is slender and dull green with bright green on the growing ends. The other kind is a denser dark green moss. It grows several inches long. In an aquarium, fountain mosses will grow in cool water and subdued light.

FLOATING PLANTS

CRYSTALWORTS either float in ponds or grow on the mud along the edge. There are two kinds. The broad kind floats on the surface; the narrow, branched kind forms a bright green network just below the surface. Some kinds of fishes lay their eggs in crystalwort. The narrow kind is sometimes sold in aquarium stores.

The MOSS FERN (*Salvinia*) floats on the water's surface or climbs over rocks. Its hairy leaves are grayish-green or pinkish. Some kinds grow wild; some are cultivated and sold in aquarium stores.

DUCKWEEDS also float on the surface. Some have small, oval, floating leaves that are green above and purplish underneath with rootlets hanging below. Some have leaves no bigger than pinheads; they float without roots. Others have green leaves about ½ inch long; they grow in a tangled net on the surface. Duckweeds increase fast and often cover large surfaces of stagnant water. In an aquarium they make good food for some fishes, tadpoles, snails, and other vegetarians.

Yellowish-brown moss

Slender fountain moss

Dense fountain moss

MOSSES

Broad crystalwort

Slender crystalwort

CRYSTALWORTS

MOSS FERN   **DUCKWEEDS**

STONEWORTS

Stoneworts grow 1 or 2 feet high on stones, sticks, sand, or mud at the bottom of a pond. Take some of the base on which they are growing when collecting them. The brittle stonewort, Chara, has whorls of needle-like, lime-covered branches along the stem. It grows in ponds and springs that are rich in lime. The slender stonewort, Nitella, has many branched, threadlike green stems. In an aquarium with plenty of light, it makes a dainty, fast-growing plant.

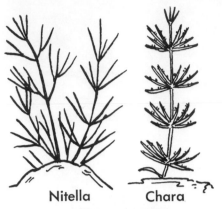

Nitella   Chara

STONEWORTS

NAIAD

This is a slender plant with narrow, threadlike leaves clustered along the stem. Small, nut-like seeds form where the leaves join the stem. This plant grows in lakes and ponds, often in deep water. If your aquarium does not get much light, this is a good plant to have.

NAIAD

WATER CLOVER FERN

The four-leaf water clover is a fern which came from abroad originally. You will find it growing wild along the muddy shores of many ponds and streams. In an aquarium it likes light and room to spread. Its roots run under the sand and send up new plants. In fall long pods, which are the fruiting part of the plant, may appear.

WATER CLOVER FERN

WATERWEED

This is a long, trailing plant with short, narrow, almost transparent leaves in groups of three or four along the stem. A cultivated kind, sold in aquarium stores, is denser and longer lived in an aquarium than a slender wild kind which grows in ponds. Give waterweed plenty of light, and it will grow for years, staying green all winter. If it becomes too thick, break off the fresh green ends and replant them, throwing out the older, brownish stems. When collecting, break off a handful of short stems. Float them in the aquarium, or you can anchor the cut ends in the sand.

WATERWEED (Elodea or Anacharis)

PONDWEEDS

Pondweeds grow rooted to the bottom of lakes and ponds; their sprawling stems reach to the surface. There are several kinds. The ruffle-leaf kind has long, thin brown or green wavy-edged leaves along the length of the stem. The slender-leaf kind has narrow leaves under water and oval, floating leaves at the surface. In shallow water you may find some pondweeds small enough to grow in an aquarium. Or you can break off short lengths of stem from larger plants. Stick the broken ends in the sand.

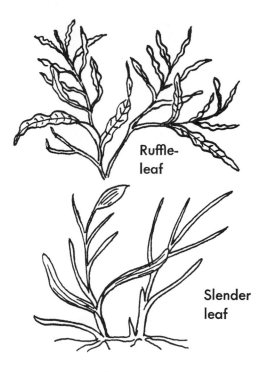

PONDWEEDS

WATER-EDGE PLANTS

Several plants which grow at the edge of ponds and streams and in damp meadows will also grow in an aquarium.

WATER CRESS grows in shallow brooks and other wet places. It has divided green leaves. A few young plants may be tried in the aquarium. Snails like to eat them.

WATER CRESS

LUDWIGIA grows at the edge of ponds, streams, and in ditches. It has long, trailing stems with small, oval leaves that grow in pairs along the stem. The leaves are light green, sometimes reddish underneath. Varieties of this plant are sold in aquarium supply stores.

One of the easiest plants to find and to grow is the MONEYWORT, or CREEPING CHARLIE. A creeping plant common in moist meadows, it has rounded leaves in pairs along a trailing stem. In spring yellow flowers bloom in pairs above the leaves. Underwater it does not flower. The land leaves turn brown and drop off, but new stems with smaller leaves grow and reach up to the surface. In an aquarium that gets some sunlight, the leaves stay green and continue to grow through the winter. Moneywort is sold as an aquarium plant in supply stores.

LUDWIGIA

On land

Under water

MONEYWORT or CREEPING CHARLIE

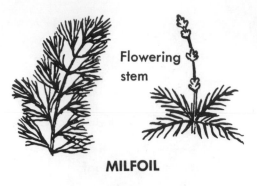

MILFOIL

Flowering stem

FANWORT (Cabomba)

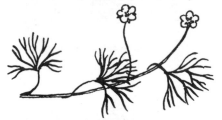

WATER BUTTERCUP

Winter bud

HORNWORT

BLADDERWORT

FEATHERY-LEAVED PLANTS

WATER MILFOIL has threadlike leaves which grow in whorls close together on the long stem. You will find it in slow streams and shallow ponds. The stem is rooted in the bottom mud, but it may grow several feet long and reach to the surface. Small, purple flowers bloom on spikes above the water. Milfoil is often sold in aquarium stores. In an aquarium it grows in moderate light. Some fishes lay eggs on its leaves.

FANWORT, OR CABOMBA, is a popular aquarium plant. Most aquarium stores keep it in stock. It grows wild in many ponds and streams, especially in the southeast. It has threadlike green leaves that form fan-shaped clusters along a trailing stem. Out of doors in summer, fanwort has small white or yellow flowers at the surface and some oval floating leaves. In an aquarium the stem may be anchored in sand or floated in water. Besides being ornamental, the plant serves as shelter and food for many fishes. Broken pieces of stem will grow into new plants.

The WATER BUTTERCUP has fan-shaped leaves which are farther apart on the stem than fanwort leaves. It grows in the shallow water of ponds and streams. The weak, trailing stems grow to be a foot long. In summer it has small, white flowers at the surface.

HORNWORT has threadlike, stiff, forked green leaves in whorls along the stem. The leaves at the growing tip form thick clusters like a coon tail, which is a common name for the plant. In autumn the plant dies back to the tip, which sinks to the bottom and lives over as a winter bud. Hornwort stems may grow several feet long. They float unrooted under the surface of ponds, often some distance from the shore. Hornwort seeds drop to the bottom where they grow into small plants. When the plants are a few inches long, they break off and float to the surface. In an aquarium hornwort will grow fast in a moderate light.

BLADDERWORT also has threadlike forked leaves and a long stem which floats under the surface without roots. It grows in stagnant water. Where the leaves fork, there are small bladders, or sacs. These are traps which catch and digest tiny water life. If a bladderwort plant is put into an aquarium which contains minute animal life, its bladders will soon become loaded.

RIBBON-LEAVED PLANTS

TAPE GRASS has long, narrow leaves which rise in bunches from the roots. It grows in the mud of ponds, lakes, and slow streams. The leaves are about ¼ inch wide, and may grow 3 feet long. In some shallow places the plants are so thick that they fill the water. In an aquarium, tape grass will grow well but not so large as out of doors. It should be planted at the back of the aquarium.

Tape grass increases by sending out runners from the base of the plant. In the pond it also forms seeds. Separate plants have male and female flowers. The male flowers are on short stems under water; when ripe, they break off and float to the surface. Small, greenish, seed-bearing female flowers open at the surface. Each one is on a long, coiled, springy stem. As the seeds form, the stem contracts and pulls them down under water. In winter the plants usually die back to the roots.

NARROW-LEAVED ARROWHEADS, or SAGITTARIA, grow in swamps and other shallow waters. The plants are from a few inches to a few feet high. Some kinds have stiff, rounded leaves; some have narrow, flat leaves. New plants form on runners sent out from the base of the plant as well as from seeds. In summer they have small, white flowers, each with three petals, in groups of three near the top of the stem. Choose small plants for the aquarium. They will not bloom, but they will send up groups of green leaves much like tape grass.

The BROAD-LEAVED ARROWHEAD has arrow-shaped leaves. It grows along the edge of ponds with its roots in the water. Small plants may be tried for a short time in an aquarium, but the leaves will soon reach above water.

STARGRASS, or MUD PLANTAIN, grows rooted in the mud of still or flowing shallow water. Its slender, forked stem may be several feet long. Grasslike leaves grow along the stem. Small, yellow flowers bloom at the surface all summer. Small plants will grow well in an aquarium which gets plenty of light.

HAIRGRASS is a dainty plant with hairlike leaves which grow from 3 to 8 inches high. It grows rooted to the muddy bottom of ponds in the middle and southern Atlantic states. In an aquarium it will make a light green mat over the bottom.

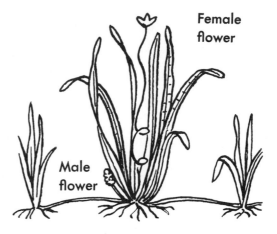

Female flower

Male flower

TAPE GRASS

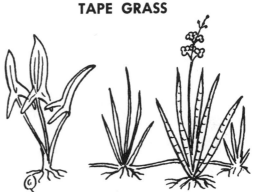

ARROWHEADS

STAR GRASS or MUD PLANTAIN

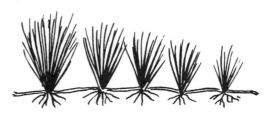

HAIR GRASS

SNAILS AND CLAMS

Snails and clams make useful additions to any aquarium. They will thrive with very little care from you, and—also important—they will help to keep your aquarium clean.

WHERE TO FIND

While plants are taking root and starting to grow in your aquarium is a good time to go out and look for some snails and clams.

Look for snails along the shallow edge of a lake, pond or stream; in the mud or rotting leaves at the bottom; under stones, sticks, or rubbish in the water; and on the leaves of water plants.

Look for the larger clams, or mussels, in mud at the bottom of shallow water. Look for tiny fingernail or pill clams in the sand or mud at the bottom of clear pools and streams, or among water plants.

HOW TO CATCH

To collect snails or clams, poke around in likely places with a strainer, scoop, or sieve.

A kitchen strainer may be attached to a long stick. Cut off part of the strainer handle and force the remaining part inside a hollow stick like a shade roller or piece of bamboo. Or leave the handle as is and bind it with wire or tape to the outside of a stick.

A scoop may be made of ¼-inch mesh hardware cloth fastened to a flat stick. See page 67 for pattern.

To make a tin can sieve, punch holes in the bottom of the can with a nail or ice pick. Punch from the inside, so that the rough part will be outside. Fasten the can to a flat stick as shown in the picture.

HOW TO CARRY

To carry the snails and clams home, use a container such as a glass jar with a metal screw top that has holes punched in it, a small pail, or a can with holes punched in the lid. Partly fill the container with pond water. Several jars or cans can be carried in a fruit basket.

HOW TO KEEP

When you get home, empty the container with its contents into your aquarium. The light and temperature in which plants will grow are suitable for snails and clams.

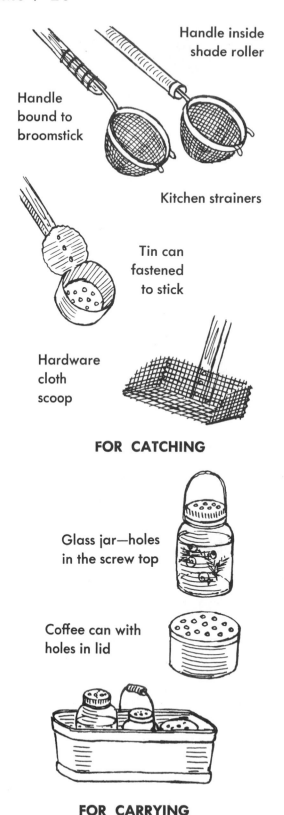

Handle inside shade roller

Handle bound to broomstick

Kitchen strainers

Tin can fastened to stick

Hardware cloth scoop

FOR CATCHING

Glass jar—holes in the screw top

Coffee can with holes in lid

FOR CARRYING

Clams feeding through siphons

Snails eating lettuce

Snails eating
algae on glass

FEEDING

Young clams

On glass   On waterweed

Snail eggs

Live-born snails

EGGS AND YOUNG

HOW TO FEED

In an aquarium snails glide over the sides and bottom and on the plants, eating the algae that are usually present. On the underside of its head a snail has a rough, filelike tongue with which it scrapes up food. Snails eat decaying as well as fresh animal and plant material, and so help to keep the aquarium clean.

If there are growing plants in the aquarium, all the extra food snails will need is a small piece of lettuce or spinach once a week and a bit of raw meat or fish once in a while. Snails cannot live in water that is too acid. If their shells show white streaks, add a lump of plaster of Paris to the water.

Clams draw their food from the water. They eat the microscopic life that it usually contains. Add pond water once in a while to renew this life.

HOW SNAILS AND CLAMS INCREASE

Most snails lay eggs; a few kinds bear young snails alive. Some kinds of snails are both male and female; some are one or the other. Usually they mate before laying eggs, but some kinds lay without mating.

Snail eggs are in jelly masses attached to leaves of water plants, sticks, stones, or rubbish in the water. In an aquarium the eggs are sometimes attached to the sides.

The large clams, or mussels, are either male or female. The female lays thousands of eggs which she carries in her gill sacs until they hatch into larval clams. The larvae are only partly developed and are unable to feed themselves. They have the curious habit of attaching themselves to fishes and feeding on the fishes' blood while they are changing into young clams. After a few weeks the young clam drops off, falls to the bottom, and draws its food from the water.

Female pill and fingernail clams each lay only a few eggs which they carry in their gill sacs until hatched. These young clams, though tiny, are developed enough to feed themselves. They do not attach to fishes. You may discover some of these young in your aquarium among the full-grown clams; they look like white dots.

PARTS OF A CLAM

A clam has two matching shells which are held together by a hinge near the top, or beak. The shells open to let two necks, or siphons, stick out on one end and a triangular-shaped foot stick out on the other end. The clam draws water into its body through one siphon and lets it out through the other one. From the water the clam gets oxygen to breathe and food to eat.

When the clam wants to move, it extends its foot, hooks it into the mud or to a plant or other support, and pulls itself along.

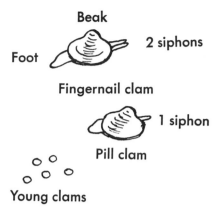

Beak

Foot   2 siphons

Fingernail clam

1 siphon

Pill clam

Young clams

KINDS OF CLAMS

A number of different kinds of clams live in fresh water. Their shells vary in size from ½ to 5 inches long, in color from almost white to dark purple or brown. Several small clams may be kept in an aquarium with other kinds of animal life.

Full-grown PILL and FINGERNAIL CLAMS are only ½ to ¾ of an inch long. Their shells are light greenish, yellowish, or brownish. Some kinds have equal shells, some are one-sided, some have caplike beaks. Fingernail clams have two short pinkish siphons and a waxy white, tongue-like foot. Pill clams have only one siphon to let water out. The water enters through a hole alongside the body.

These little clams are more active than the larger ones. In an aquarium they glide over the bottom and climb over the plants.

SMALL CLAMS

Large clams, or MUSSELS, usually stay anchored. Their elliptical shells are from 3 to 5 inches long. On the outside the shells are dark greenish, brownish, or purplish. Some are thick and rough, some are thin and smooth. Inside they have a pearly lining. These clams have short siphons. They have a broad, flat foot which usually sticks out of the partly opened shell and is often partly buried in the mud.

One large clam is enough to keep in a large aquarium with other creatures. Or keep one or two by themselves in a container with pond water. Watch that the clam stays alive. If its shell gapes wide open, it is dead and should be removed at once.

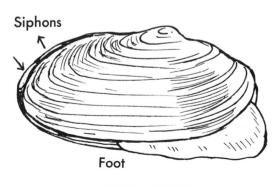

Siphons

Foot

LARGE MUSSEL

PARTS OF A SNAIL

Tentacles
Mouth
Foot
Shell

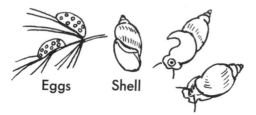

Eggs Shell

TADPOLE SNAIL

Laying eggs

SMALLER POND SNAIL

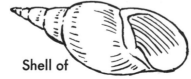

Shell of
LARGER POND SNAIL

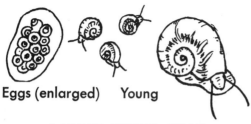

Eggs (enlarged) Young

LARGER WHEEL SNAIL

LIMPETS

Snails of various shapes and sizes live in fresh water. They are easily raised and are quite useful in an aquarium, but they are not always easy to find.

PARTS OF A SNAIL

A snail has a spiral shell with a right- or left-hand opening. Its body is twisted like the shell and can be drawn inside. When the snail moves, it extends the lower part of its body and glides on the flat underside, or foot. It has two feelers, or tentacles, and a small, black eye at the base of each. Its mouth, on the underside, has a filelike tongue with small teeth, or hooks, to scrape up the food.

EGG-LAYING, AIR-BREATHING SNAILS

These snails rise to the surface to breathe air which they take into a lung sac. They can hold enough air to last them for some time.

TADPOLE SNAILS *(Physa)* are common in most ponds. In an aquarium they are hardy, active, and increase fast. They have shiny, brown shells that grow ½ inch long and have a left-hand opening. They glide around the aquarium on a foot with a pointed end. In spring and summer they lay many eggs in small blobs of jelly on stems, leaves, or other support.

POND SNAILS *(Lymnaea)* have long, light or dark brown shells with a right-hand opening. A small kind grows to be 1 inch long, a larger kind 2 or more inches. In spring and summer these snails lay eggs in long jelly masses on leaves or something else in water.

WHEEL SNAILS have a spiral shell that is flattened on each side. It is brownish, rough or smooth, rounded or angular. Some small kinds are ¼ inch or less across. The largest wheel snail is about 1 inch across. In an aquarium it often lays eggs on the glass sides. The eggs are in a yellowish jelly mass. With a magnifying glass you can see the young snails developing in the eggs.

LIMPETS are very small snails with low cone-shaped shells. They glide on an oval-shaped foot over plants, stones, and the glass sides of the aquarium. Besides a lung sac, they also have a gill.

LIVE-BEARING, WATER-BREATHING SNAILS

These snails breathe oxygen from the water through gills. They do not have to rise to the surface. They can withdraw into their shells and seal themselves in with a horny plate, or operculum, which fits the opening like a door. The operculum is carried on the back of the foot when the snail is partly out of its shell. When the snail withdraws into its shell, it doubles its foot under and pulls it in from the back. This brings the operculum up last to cover the shell opening.

Instead of laying eggs these snails bear their young alive.

The GREENISH SNAIL (*Ambloxis*) may be found in the shallow part of rivers and streams. It is not easy to find because it usually burrows in sand or mud at the bottom. Its shell grows an inch or more long and is greenish or olive underneath a brown coating. It has six whorls, but the top ones are usually worn off. The snail has a wide, flat, pinkish foot and short, pointed tentacles.

Large, rounded POND SNAILS (*Viviparus*) live on the muddy bottom of ponds, lakes, and rivers. Their globular shell grows 2 inches or more long. One kind has a brown or olive shell with dark bands; another kind has a purplish shell; another has a dark brown ridged shell.

These snails have a large, flat, speckled brown and black foot and a large, cone-shaped head. They have long, pointed tentacles. You can tell the male from the female by looking at the tentacles; the right tentacle of the male is shorter and almost as broad as the head.

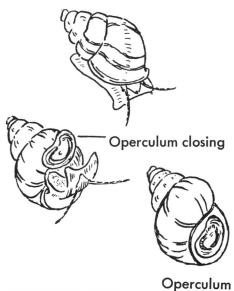

Operculum closing

GREENISH SNAIL

Operculum closed

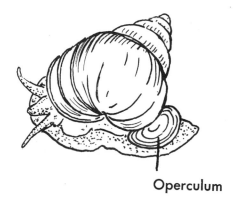

Operculum

LARGE ROUNDED POND SNAIL

In jelly sac (enlarged)

Young snails

Snails bearing young alive

FISHES

Fishes are always interesting pets for an aquarium. Wild fishes, which you can catch yourself, are often as colorful and attractive as those you can buy at an aquarium store.

WHERE TO FIND

With plants and snails in the aquarium, it is ready for some fish.

Look for small fish in ponds, the shallow edge of lakes, slow streams, and brooks. Fish from swift streams usually will not live in an aquarium which does not have running or aerated water.

Minnows may be taken wherever fishing is allowed, but the young of game fish should be taken only where state game laws permit.

HOW TO CATCH

Catch fish with a cloth, not metal, net. You can use a landing net with fine mesh, or you can make a net. For a homemade net, use mosquito netting, curtain material, or other fine netting. To make the net less conspicuous, light material should be dyed dark green or brown. Strong tea may be used as a dye. Cut a piece of netting about 16 inches deep and wide enough to fit around the frame. Using strong thread, sew the side and bottom seams; then sew the net to the frame. Tape sewed over the seams and frame will make the net stronger.

The frame may be made from a wire coat hanger in its natural shape, or pulled out to make a circle or rectangle. Straighten out the hook or cut it off. Then insert the hook end into a hollow stick or fasten it to the outside of a stick with wire or screws. For a stick you can use a bamboo pole, a shade roller, or broomstick.

When using the net, try sweeping it downward through the water, pulling it toward your feet.

A shallow net baited with corn bread, cracker crumbs, or other fish food may be tried. Lower it at a place where minnows collect. These nets can be hooked over the end of a stick or hung from a wire or string.

If many small fish are needed, a hand seine may be used if the game laws permit. The seine is a long strip of netting, 2 or 3 feet wide, fastened to a pole at each end. Two people, each holding a pole, walk along a stream drawing the net through the water.

When fishing, be prepared to wade in the water by wearing boots or sneakers or going barefoot.

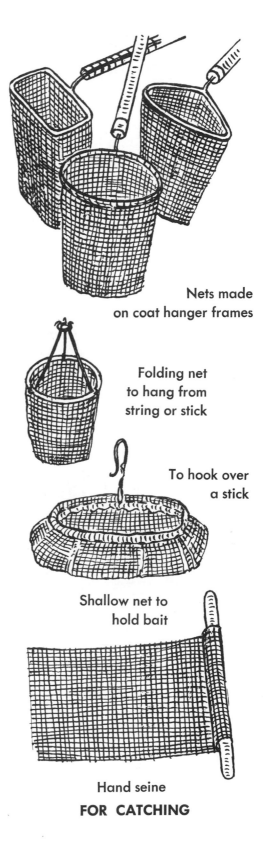

Nets made
on coat hanger frames

Folding net
to hang from
string or stick

To hook over
a stick

Shallow net to
hold bait

Hand seine
FOR CATCHING

Netting on top
held by rubber band

Netting in
screw rim

Lid with
holes

Glass jars

Enamel pail

FOR CARRYING

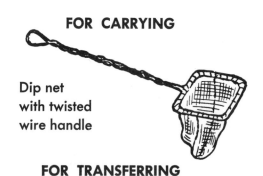

Dip net
with twisted
wire handle

FOR TRANSFERRING

HOW TO CARRY

To carry the fish home, use glass jars or an enamel or plastic pail; a metal container might poison the water. If jars are used, fill ¾ full of pond water and cover with netting or a screw top with holes punched in it. A string around the top of the jar will make a handle. Several jars may be carried in a box or basket. It is better to put only one kind of fish in each container and only a few of that kind. If the fish are too crowded, they will die.

At home, carefully empty each jar with its water and fish into the aquarium. To transfer the fish from a large container to the aquarium, use a small dip net. You can buy one in an aquarium store, or you can make one from copper wire and thin cloth like lawn or organdy.

If you transfer fish by hand, have your hands wet and be careful not to rub off any scales or the protective slime that coats the fish.

HOW TO KEEP

Keep only as many fish as will live comfortably in your aquarium; about 1 inch of fish to one or two gallons of water is a good rule. A six-gallon aquarium could have three to six 1-inch fish, or two or three 2-inch fish.

Do not put aggressive kinds of fish with other kinds or with smaller fish of the same kind. By watching different kinds of fish in an aquarium for a day or two, you can tell whether they will get along well together.

For kinds of containers that may be used as aquariums, see page 11.

Keep the aquarium in a light window where it will get about two hours of sunlight in winter, less or none in summer. If the aquarium must be in a very sunny window, put a piece of cardboard over the top or between it and the window. Avoid sudden changes in temperature; in winter do not have the aquarium near a hot radiator or an open window.

It is better for the fish not to have the water changed often. If there are growing plants, and if leftover food and other decaying matter is removed by siphon (see page 13) every day or two, the water may not need changing more than twice a year.

SICK FISH

Before putting new fish into the aquarium, look for signs of sickness. If the fish look unhealthy, return them to the pond, or keep them in a tank by themselves and treat them for sickness. If a fish in the aquarium becomes sick, it should be removed at once and put into a separate container.

These are all signs of sickness: sluggishness, loss of appetite, loss of balance, shaking, drooping fins, ragged tail, white slime on body or around mouth, white or dark woolly patches, white or dark spots on body, puffiness or thinness, gasping at the surface. A gasping fish may not really be sick; it may not be getting enough oxygen from the water because the aquarium is overcrowded or needs fresh water.

TREATMENT FOR SICKNESS

Most sick fish will benefit from a salt water bath. Use shallow water at room temperature. Add salt in the amount of one teaspoonful to a gallon of water. Sea salt or rock salt is best, but table salt with a pinch of Epsom salt may be used. Make a fresh solution each day for four days and keep the fish in it continuously, if necessary. If the fish is not better then, make a stronger solution of one tablespoonful of salt to a gallon of water and keep the fish in it for a half hour or longer (up to two days). Then you may put it back in the weaker solution for a few days if necessary.

Instead of salt, 2 per cent Mercurochrome may be used for sicknesses like white spots or sores. Add three or four drops to a gallon of water each day; keep the fish in it for three days. A fish with a sore spot may be caught in a soft net and the spot can be painted with Mercurochrome on a cotton swab.

A tank of green water is a good tonic for a convalescing fish. The fish may be kept in it a week or so. Green water is found in stagnant pools, also in an aquarium which has been kept in a sunny window. The color comes from tiny plants (algae) growing in the water. Do not use the water if it turns brown, since that means the plants have died.

Fish diseases are not caught by humans.

Gasping at surface

Drooping fins

Ragged tail

Woolly patches

Slimy mouth

White spots

SIGNS OF SICKNESS

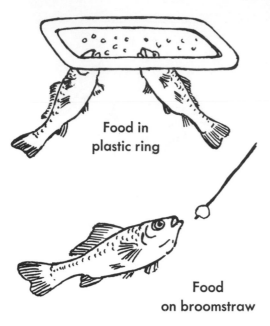

Food in
plastic ring

Food
on broomstraw

The lean,
hungry look

On bottom
of aquarium

FEEDING

WHAT TO FEED

Wild fish eat insects, crustaceans, smaller fish, worms, other small animal life, and some plant stuff. In an aquarium, fish will eat a number of things; they like variety in their food. See that the meat-eaters get enough animal food; only a few kinds of fish are vegetarians.

FOOD FOR OLDER FISH

Cereal foods: pablum, cornmeal, farina, boiled oatmeal, ground puppy biscuit, graham cracker crumbs.

Leafy foods: duckweed and other water plants, chopped lettuce, chopped lightly-cooked spinach.

Animal foods: shredded dry or fresh shrimp including some shell, shredded crab, finely chopped raw clam or oyster; raw or cooked fish, dried fish roe; raw or lightly-cooked liver; raw lean beef; crumbled hard-boiled egg yolk; cottage cheese; dried insects; freshly-killed flies.

Live animal foods: tiny crustaceans such as water fleas that look like tiny white specks in the water; water insects including mosquito wrigglers; small snails; tubifex and other water worms (washed free of dirt), earthworms.

Prepared fish foods usually contain a mixture of dry animal and cereal food. Buy it finely ground for baby fish, medium for small fish, coarse for large fish.

FOOD FOR BABY FISH

Newly hatched fish may be fed water containing microscopic animal and plant life (infusoria). Infusoria are in most water which has been exposed to air, including aquarium water. To grow more infusoria, put a little dried hay or lettuce leaves in a jar. Fill the jar with hot water and let it stand in a warm place in subdued light for a few days. Then it may be added, a teaspoon at a time, to the aquarium.

After the fish are two or three weeks old, they may be fed the following foods: prepared fish food, finely ground; strained cooked oatmeal; farina; blood from beef; juice from clam; mashed beef liver with pablum; fish roe; scraped raw beef; shredded boiled fish; strained hard-boiled egg yolk; tiny crustaceans.

WHEN TO FEED

Feed adult and partly-grown fish once a day; or if they do not seem hungry, every other day. In winter fish may eat less. Put the food into the aquarium a little at a time and see that each fish gets a share. A few mouthfuls is enough for each fish. If it is necessary to leave the aquarium without care for a few days, the fish will not starve, especially if there are growing plants and minute animal life in the water.

The best time to feed fish is in the morning. Then un-eaten food may be removed from the bottom at night with a dip tube or siphon.

HOW TO FEED

Cereal food may be sprinkled sparingly on the surface. Or you may buy a plastic feeding ring from an aquarium store and put the food in the center of it to prevent it from spreading over the surface.

Growing plants should be in the water all the time, if possible. Lettuce and spinach may be dropped into the water in very small amounts when the fish are feeding.

Live animal food may be put into the water in small amounts at any time, since it will live until eaten.

Animal food, like bits of meat, fish, or pieces of earth-worm, may be dropped into the water in small amounts when the fish are hungry. Or small pieces may be put on the end of a broomstraw or string and lowered into the water in front of the fish. Some tame fish will jump out of the water for food. Some learn to come to the surface and feed from one's fingers.

Some kinds of fish feed on the bottom and clean up food dropped by the other fish. However, they shouldn't be depended on to keep the aquarium clean. Uneaten food should be removed before it has a chance to decay.

Baby fish need to be fed oftener than older fish—up to five or six times a day. Add a teaspoonful of infusoria water to the aquarium about six times a day. As the fish grow, add tiny crustaceans, such as water fleas, to the aquarium; and several times a day drop in bits of other baby fish food. Watch that the water does not become foul.

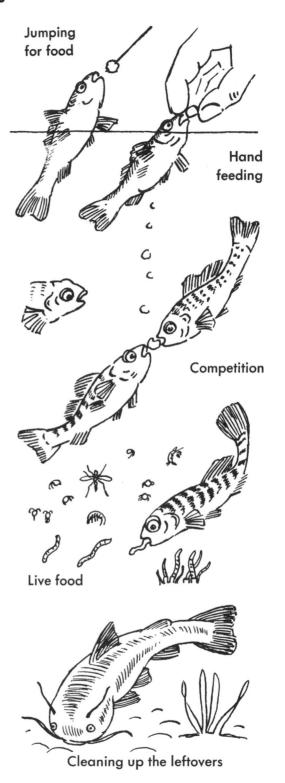

Jumping for food

Hand feeding

Competition

Live food

Cleaning up the leftovers

FEEDING

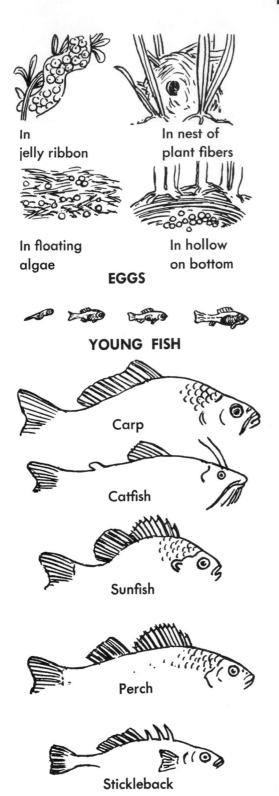

In
jelly ribbon

In nest of
plant fibers

In floating
algae

In hollow
on bottom

EGGS

YOUNG FISH

Carp

Catfish

Sunfish

Perch

Stickleback

KINDS OF FISHES

HOW FISH LIVE

Fish breathe oxygen dissolved in the water. They take the water in through their mouths and pass it over their gills where the oxygen is absorbed. The water flows out through the gill opening.

Fish see with their eyes, which always stay open. They hear and help to keep balanced with their ears, which are hidden inside their head. They smell but do not breathe with their nostrils. Other sense organs are in their skin, including the lateral line which seems to sense vibrations. They use their fins for swimming.

HOW FISH INCREASE

Most female fish lay eggs; only a few kinds bear their young alive. The eggs are usually laid in spring, often in some kind of a nest made by the male. Some females lay their eggs on plant leaves or masses of algae. The female perch lays her eggs in a zigzag string of jelly draped around a water plant. After the eggs are laid, the male fish fertilizes them by pouring a fluid over them. The eggs hatch into tiny fish which are mostly transparent except for their stomachs and eyes.

HOW TO TELL KINDS OF FISHES APART

To tell one kind of fish from another, look at its general shape, its mouth, head, skin, and fins. You cannot always tell the kind of fish by its color, as the color may vary with its surroundings and its age.

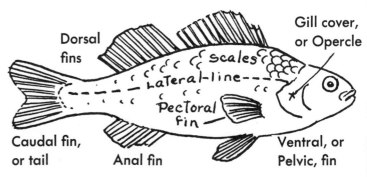

Dorsal
fins

Gill cover,
or Opercle

scales

Lateral-line

Pectoral
fin

Caudal fin,
or tail

Anal fin

Ventral, or
Pelvic, fin

PARTS OF A FISH

KINDS OF FISHES

There are many kinds of small, wild fishes which may be kept in an aquarium. They are as interesting and often as pretty as the fishes that are sold in pet stores. Wild fishes are easier to raise because they do not need a heated aquarium and they are usually not fussy about their food. Wild carp and minnows are relatives of the goldfish.

GOLDFISH

Sometimes goldfish are put into a pond where they live and increase like wild fishes. The female goldfish lays her eggs on the leaves and stems of water plants. The male swims over the eggs and fertilizes them. In a week or less the eggs hatch into tiny black fish. It is several months before the young fish become brightly colored. If several generations of goldfish have lived in the pond, the young fish may remain dark colored all their lives.

In an aquarium goldfish eat almost any kind of food including cereals, bits of vegetables, raw meat, earthworms, and prepared fish food.

CARP

Carp live in muddy ponds and lakes all over the country. They are reddish-gold, olive-brown, or silvery, sometimes with tinges of yellow or pink. They are humpbacked, have coarse scales, and one long dorsal fin. Adult carp grow 2 feet or more long. Young carp are light silvery or golden and less humpbacked than the adults. They are a good size for the aquarium when they are an inch or two long. Larger carp might uproot plants and stir up the sand when they feed on the bottom.

Carp eat both animal and plant food; in an aquarium they especially like bits of raw meat or fish and pieces of worm. They will learn to take food from a straw or from one's fingers.

Baby carp hatch in spring from eggs laid in shallow water, often among plant roots and stems. The young carp grow faster than most fishes; by fall they may be from 3 to 5 inches long. In an aquarium fish rarely grow as fast as they do out of doors.

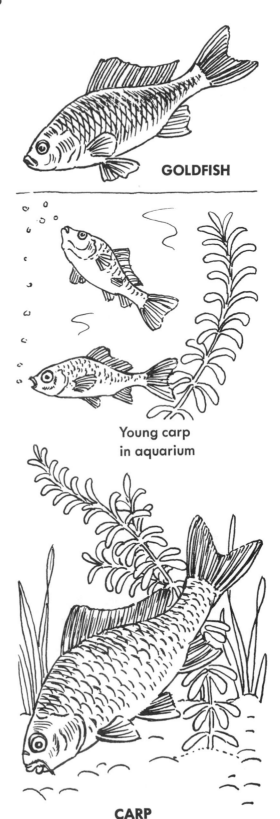

GOLDFISH

Young carp
in aquarium

CARP

GOLDEN SHINER

COMMON SHINER

REDFIN SHINER

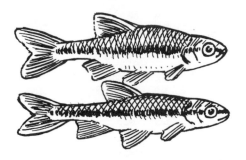

**BLACKCHIN AND
BLACKNOSE SHINERS**

BLUNT-NOSED MINNOW

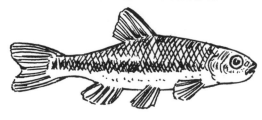

CUTLIPS MINNOW

MINNOWS

Minnows, of which there are several kinds, belong to the same family as carp and goldfish. They are small, slender fish, common in most ponds and streams. Fishermen often use them for bait. Many of them have bright, iridescent coloring which is most attractive in an aquarium. Most of them are hardy and easy to raise. If you have goldfish, you could try putting one or two minnows with them. Or keep several minnows in an aquarium by themselves. They like rather cool water and growing plants. They eat most kinds of fish food including prepared food (medium ground), bits of raw meat, earthworms, and a variety of small insects such as mosquito larvae.

GOLDEN SHINERS grow to be 12 inches long. They are bright golden or silvery when adult. Young shiners are greenish-brown on the back, and silvery with a dark line on the sides.

The COMMON SHINER grows to be 8 to 10 inches long. It is silvery on the sides and bluish or greenish on the back. In breeding season (May or June) the male has small bumps on his head and a rosy color on the lower fins and belly.

The REDFIN SHINER grows to be about 3½ inches long. In spring the male is colorful with dark blue on the back, silvery and greenish-blue on the sides with a dark band. The fins and belly are bright red.

BLACKCHIN and BLACKNOSE SHINERS are silvery with a black band running from mouth to tail. In the blackchin the black goes over the chin; in the blacknose, over the nose. These shiners grow to be about 2½ inches long.

The BLUNT-NOSED MINNOW grows to be 4 inches. It is olive on the back and bluish on the sides. In spring the male's head is black, and he has small bumps on the head and back. The male guards the eggs which the female lays on the underside of stones.

The CUTLIPS MINNOW grows to be 8 inches. Its lower jaw is divided into three lobes, making it look a little as if it had the mumps. It is dark colored, the male being nearly black on the back in the spring breeding season. He makes a pebble nest, usually under a stone, in which one or more females lay their yellow eggs.

MORE MINNOWS

Dace are pretty minnows which are found in many brooks and streams. They make fine aquarium pets since they get along well with other fishes. They eat most kinds of fish food including prepared food, dried shrimp, tiny insects and small earthworms. They grow to be about 3 inches long. Keep them in fairly cool water and give them plenty of swimming space.

BLACK-NOSE DACE

BLACK-NOSE DACE are dark silvery on the back, and light underneath with a dark line from nose to tail. The breeding male has some orange-red underneath. Although these dace live in flowing streams, they will also often live for years in an aquarium if it is not crowded.

RED-BELLY DACE

RED-BELLY DACE are so colorful that they are sometimes sold in pet shops. They are olive on the back and silvery or golden with two black bands on the sides. In spring and summer the males are red on the sides and underneath. The females lay eggs in masses of thread algae (fine, floating green plant stuff). Algae and insects are among the natural food of these dace. The northern red-belly lives in bogs, ponds, and streams; the southern kind lives in clear, gravelly streams.

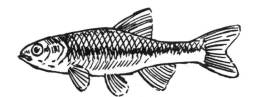

ROSY-SIDED DACE

ROSY-SIDED DACE are silvery or greenish on the back with a black band along the sides. The males have a rosy patch underneath which is brightest in spring and summer. These dace live in cool brooks in the eastern states south of New York.

BANDED KILLIFISH

BANDED KILLIFISH are small minnows (up to 3 inches long) which are common in ponds, lakes, and brackish water especially where there are rushes, grasses, and other water plants. In summer the females lay eggs among the plants in shallow water.

These killifish are silvery and they have dark up-and-down bars on the sides instead of horizontal stripes as in most fishes. Out of doors, they eat small crustaceans, insects, algae, and plant seeds. In captivity they will also eat medium-ground fish food and tiny bits of meat or earthworms.

As they usually feed near the surface, they have upturned mouths. In an aquarium they may learn to leap for food on the end of a straw. They become very tame, and may live for years.

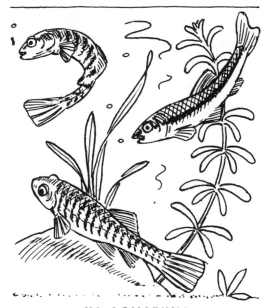

IN AQUARIUM

STONEROLLERS

MUD MINNOWS

BOTTOM MINNOWS

STONEROLLER MINNOWS live in shallow brooks and streams among the mud and gravel at the bottom. They eat ooze and other vegetable stuff, rolling small stones about to get at their food. In an aquarium, they like to have some small stones on the bottom and some growing plants. They will clean algae off the bottom and sides. Give them leafy foods to eat.

The stoneroller minnow grows 6 to 8 inches long. It has thick lips on the underside of its head like the sucker fishes. In color it is olive-brown with darker markings on the sides. It has a dark bar behind the opercle and on the dorsal fin and a dark spot at the base of the tail. In spring the fins of the breeding male are bright orange or red and his body is covered with small bumps. He makes a hollow nest by pushing some of the bottom gravel aside, and the female lays her eggs in it. Except when defending its nest, the stoneroller is peaceful and may be kept with other fishes in an aquarium.

The MUD MINNOW lives at the bottom of streams, swamps, and ditches, often among water plants, in most of the eastern states. Sometimes it is sold in aquarium stores. It grows 4 or 5 inches long. Along its side it has light and dark olive-brown stripes with a dark bar at the base of the tail. The color varies in different localities.

When in danger this minnow wriggles down into the bottom mud, tail first, until it is almost hidden. It also burrows into the mud if the water in its pond gets very low. In this way it is able to survive where other fishes would perish. Often it is the only fish living in shallow ponds, bogs, and swamps. It will live in an aquarium with a layer of mud in the bottom, cool water, and shaded light. It eats animal food including smaller fishes, so it is usually better to keep only one in an aquarium. In summer it may not eat as much as in cool weather.

Out of doors the mud minnow sometimes jumps out of the water to catch insects. In an aquarium it may be trained to jump for a bit of raw meat on the end of a string or straw. When not feeding the fish, keep the aquarium covered so that it will not jump out. Sometimes the fish rests in the water with its body stiff and only its fins moving.

DARTERS AND PERCH

Darters are small fish like the minnows, but they are not related to them. They belong to the perch family. They have a double dorsal fin and large pectoral fins.

JOHNNY DARTERS are olive-brown with darker markings on body and fins. They grow about 3 inches long. In spring, at breeding time, the males are darker in color. The females lay eggs on the underside of stones.

Johnny darters live at the bottom of brooks and streams. They are not easy to catch because they dart off in unexpected directions when anyone approaches. Sometimes they may be caught in a net stretched across the bottom. Although they prefer running water, they may live in an aquarium with a wide-open top, cool, rather shallow water, and water plants. They eat small live animal food, bits of raw meat, and some algae.

In an aquarium, Johnny darters are amusing to watch. With their front fins they climb among water plants, cling to the glass, or rest on the bottom. They can turn their heads to look around with their large, bulging eyes.

The RAINBOW DARTER is a brightly colored variety which lives in some clear brooks and streams. It is sometimes sold in aquarium stores. In spring and summer the male has blue bars and orange spots on the sides, orange underneath, and orange and blue on the fins. The female is much duller. Adult fish are 2½ inches long and are stouter bodied than the Johnny darter. They are not very easy to raise because they prefer aerated or running water and live animal food.

YELLOW PERCH are game fish common in many lakes, ponds, and large streams. They are dark on the back, yellow with dark bars on the sides, white underneath with orange lower fins. Small perch may be taken for the aquarium where game laws permit. Feed them animal food, such as earthworms, raw meat, and prepared fish food.

In March, April, and May, perch lay eggs in long, zigzag jelly ribbons wrapped around water plants. If you find some eggs and want to hatch them, put a small portion of the egg ribbon into a glass jar or bowl filled with pond water. Keep the jar in a light place. With a strong magnifying glass you can watch the fish forming inside the eggs. They hatch in about twenty days.

JOHNNY DARTER

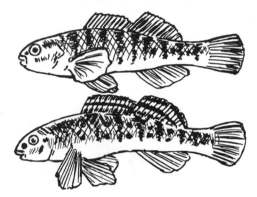

RAINBOW DARTERS

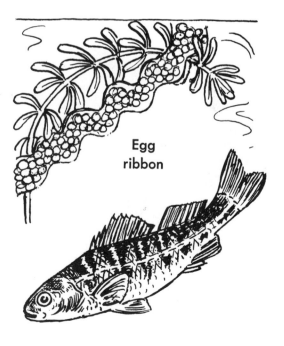

Egg ribbon

YELLOW PERCH

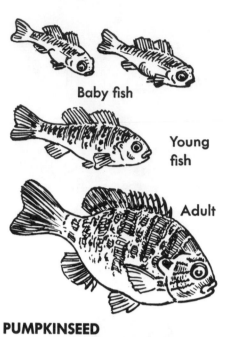

Baby fish

Young fish

Adult

PUMPKINSEED

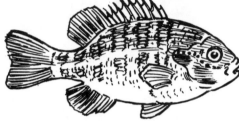

BLUEGILL

LITTLE SPOTTED

BLACK-BANDED

SUNFISH

SUNFISH

Sunfish are short, rather flat, deep-bodied fish with a long dorsal fin that is spiny in the front section. Some kinds have a conspicuous "ear" flap (opercle). One kind or another is common in ponds and lakes throughout the country.

In spring sunfish lay their eggs where the water is shallow in a hollow nest on the bottom. The nest is made and protected by the male fish. Young sunfish are colorful and easily raised in an aquarium. They eat well and will take most kinds of animal food including raw meat, fish, and pieces of earthworm. They quickly learn to feed from a broomstraw or from the fingers. As most kinds of sunfish are too aggressive to mix well with other fishes, it is usually better to keep them in a tank by themselves.

PUMPKINSEED (so called because of their shape) grow 8 inches long. They are iridescent blue and green with orange spots and dark bars on the sides and yellow or orange underneath. The "ear" flap is black with a red spot. Young ones, 1 to 3 inches long, are golden-greenish with yellow or orange spots; smaller ones are silvery.

The BLUEGILL grows larger than the pumpkinseed. It is less spotted and is orange or reddish underneath.

Little SPOTTED SUNFISHES are found along the central Atlantic Coast in ponds overgrown with plant life, creeks, and swamps. They grow about 3 inches long. One kind is dark olive-green with light bluish spots and orange underneath; another kind has reddish or yellow spots and blue-edged "ear" flaps.

The BLACK-BANDED SUNFISH, which is silvery or yellowish with black bands, grows 3 or 4 inches long. It is found from New Jersey to South Carolina in sluggish water with dense plant growth, often in cedar swamps. As it likes acid water, take a pailful of its native water when you catch the fish. This can be put into the aquarium and a little aerated tap water added as needed. Take some water plants also.

The black-banded sunfish is subject to a fungus disease. To help prevent the disease, handle the fish carefully, and do not crowd it when carrying it or keeping it. Also avoid sudden changes of water temperature. This fish is peaceful in an aquarium with other kinds of fishes.

STICKLEBACK

Stickleback are small fish which have a row of sharp spines on their back. They grow 1½ to 2½ inches long. In color they are silver-gray or brownish on the back and lighter underneath. In the spring breeding season, the males are reddish underneath with blue and green tinges on the sides.

The male fish make the nest. Some kinds use threads of algae, some use bits of leaves, and others use stems or fibers of water plants. The nests are usually rounded with a hole in one or both sides; they are attached to plant stems or lie on the bottom. The male fish coaxes one or more females into the nest. Then, after she lays her eggs, he guards the nest. He keeps the eggs aerated by fanning water over them with his fins.

If you can catch a pair of stickleback in spring, you may be able to watch them build a nest. Give them a fairly large aquarium with plenty of water plants. After the young hatch, move the parents to another tank to keep them from eating the young ones.

Feed the young infusoria (see page 33) at first, then tiny crustaceans such as water fleas and other tiny water life and fine fish food. Adult fish will eat animal food, preferably alive; algae; and a little cereal food.

Stickleback live in both salt and fresh water among water plants. Different kinds have a different number of spines on their back.

The TWO-SPINED lives in salt, or slightly salt (brackish) water along the coast. It can live in a fresh-water aquarium.

The THREE-SPINED lives both in salt and fresh water; it may go up streams in spring to lay its eggs. It will live in a fresh-water aquarium.

The FOUR-SPINED lives along the coast and in marshes, going up creeks and rivers in spring. It will live in an aquarium in brackish (somewhat salty) water.

The FIVE-SPINED, or BROOK, STICKLEBACK lives in small streams. It will live and build a nest in a fresh-water aquarium.

The NINE-SPINED lives in salt water and the shallow water of lakes, and marshes; also in a fresh-water aquarium.

BROOK

THREE-SPINED

NINE-SPINED

STICKLEBACK

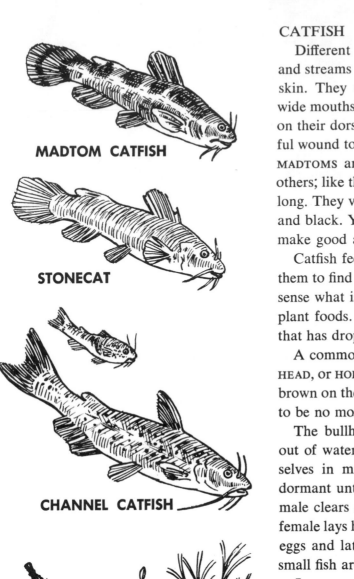

MADTOM CATFISH

STONECAT

CHANNEL CATFISH

CATFISH

Different kinds of catfish live in ponds, lakes, rivers and streams all over the country. All catfish have smooth skin. They all have whiskers, or barbels, around their wide mouths. Sharp, and in some kinds poisonous, spines on their dorsal and pectoral fins are able to cause a painful wound to anyone handling them. Some kinds, like the MADTOMS and STONECATS, are only a few inches long; others; like the CHANNEL CATFISH, grow to be several feet long. They vary in color from grayish to yellowish-brown and black. Young ones 1 to 3 inches long of any variety make good aquarium fish.

Catfish feed on the bottom. Their lower whiskers help them to find food while their upper whiskers help them to sense what is going on above. They eat both animal and plant foods. In an aquarium they help to clean up food that has dropped to the bottom.

A common catfish found in ponds is the brown BULL-HEAD, or HORNED POUT. It has a wide head and is black or brown on the back and light underneath. Usually it grows to be no more than a foot long.

The bullhead is very hardy and can live for a while out of water. In winter these fish sometimes bury themselves in mud and leaves along the shoreline and lie dormant until warmer weather. In spring or summer the male clears a round nest in the bottom gravel where the female lays her eggs. The male, or both parents, guard the eggs and later swim with the school of young fish. The small fish are coal black and look like little tadpoles.

In an aquarium, young catfish eat most kinds of food; bits of raw meat, fish, earthworm, and crumbs of dog biscuit are especially good. Do not put much smaller fish with the catfish or they may eat them.

Young fish

Adult fish

Baby fish

BULLHEAD or HORNED POUT

SUCKERS AND EELS

Suckers live in ponds and streams. They have rounded mouths with thick lips on the underside of their heads with which they suck up their food from the bottom mud.

The WHITE SUCKER grows to 20 inches long. It is dark gray or olive on the back, lighter on the sides, and white underneath. In the spring breeding season, the males are very dark on the back and have a red tinge on the fins. The females lay eggs in shallow water, burying them in loose gravel. The eggs hatch into young fish which do not have a sucking mouth until they are over 2 inches long. Try to find 3- or 4-inch suckers for your aquarium. Give them a layer of mud in the bottom and some well-anchored plants. Feed them animal food, such as raw meat, worms, coarse fish food and a little cereal food.

The LAKE CHUB SUCKER grows to be about 10 inches long. It is greenish-brown on the back, yellowish on the sides, white underneath. The young fish have a black band from nose to tail. Young chub suckers will live in an aquarium on leafy food and prepared fish food.

EELS are curious snakelike fish which grow to be several feet long. They are brownish on the back and light underneath. A small eel may be kept in a large aquarium with plants and possibly other fish. (It may nibble at the fishes' fins.) It sometimes hides by day and pokes about the bottom at night looking for food.

It will eat any kind of animal food—living, dead, or decayed—and so is a good scavenger. It may even become tame enough to feed from the hand. When it grows too big for the aquarium it should be returned to the place where it was found or to some other stream.

American eels lay their eggs far away in the Atlantic Ocean. In spring, young eels leave the ocean and start up rivers and streams. They may even wriggle overland since they can live out of water for many hours.

Sucker mouth
on underside of head

WHITE SUCKER

EEL

LAKE CHUB SUCKER

TADPOLES AND FROGS

Tadpoles will help to keep the aquarium clean. You will find them exceedingly easy to raise, and will enjoy watching them gradually change from tadpoles into frogs.

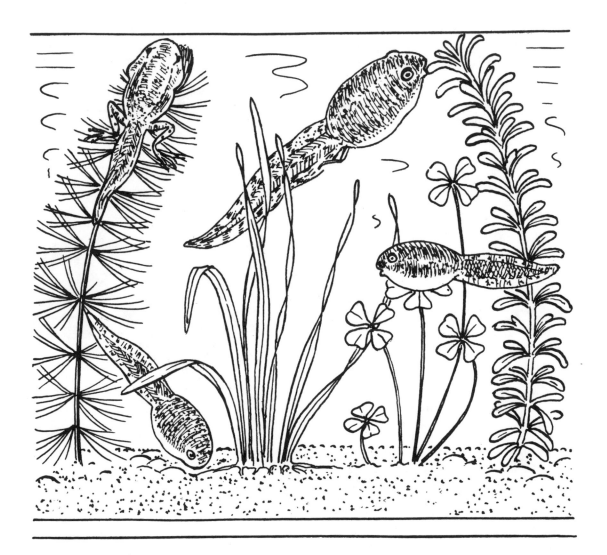

In your aquarium with plants, snails, and fishes, you may want to keep a tadpole or two. Tadpoles help to keep the aquarium clean and are amusing to watch. Tadpoles that are ready to change into frogs should be kept in an aquarium by themselves.

WHERE TO FIND

From early spring until summer you may find frog eggs among the plants in shallow water along the shore. In spring and summer you will find tadpoles in the same places. During summer and fall you will find small frogs.

HOW TO CATCH

To catch tadpoles, use a small-meshed net. The same net may be used for catching young frogs in the water. On land, you may be able to catch a frog by hand. If you can get between the frog and the water, you may have better luck than the boy in the picture. Very small frogs, which are the best size for an aquarium, are often less wary than large ones.

HOW TO CARRY

To carry tadpoles home, use a jar or can with a netting top, a lid with holes, or a pail. Partly fill the container with water and add a little green scum or a water plant for the tadpoles to eat.

Small frogs may be carried in the same kind of a container or in a cloth or net bag. It is not necessary to have them in water, but do not leave them out of water long enough to let their skins dry out. A lining of wet moss in the container is helpful.

Frog eggs should be carried in a jar, can, or pail with enough water to cover them.

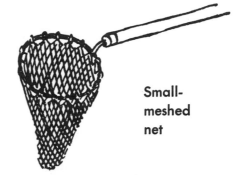

Small-meshed net

FOR CATCHING

Jars and cans

Net or cloth bag

FOR CARRYING

How to catch a frog—maybe!

FROG EGGS IN BOWL

AQUARIUMS FOR TADPOLES AND FROGS

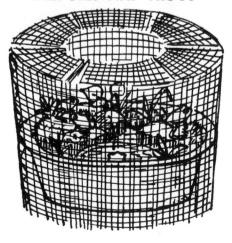

DISHPAN FROG POND

HOW TO KEEP

Frog eggs may be kept in an aquarium, a glass bowl or jar, an enamel basin, or some other container. Keep them in the pond water in which they were carried home. Add a few water plants and set the container in a window where it will get sun part of the day. The eggs of the common frogs hatch in a few days or, at the most, three weeks. If the egg mass turns white, it shows that the eggs are not developing.

After the tadpoles begin to hatch, keep only as many as you need. Remove the rest of the egg mass before it has a chance to decompose and foul the water.

Tadpoles may be kept in any of the containers shown on pages 10 and 11. Choose one that is large enough to give them room to swim around and to allow for their growing bigger.

To keep tadpoles that are changing into frogs, a container that holds part land and part water is needed. You can divide the aquarium by placing a piece of glass across it. On one side of the glass put some pebbles, soil, and sod. On the other side put some stones at the base of the glass to hold it in place. Then fill with water to within an inch of the top of the glass. Or you can make a dry place by piling up stones until they rise above the water. A piece of sod or moss can be laid on top of the stones. A piece of screen, which can be removed at feeding time, should be put across the top.

Young frogs may be kept in the same kind of part-water-and-part-land aquarium. Or you can make a miniature frog pond out of a dishpan or wash basin. Make a border of stones around the sides of the pan. Put clumps of grass or moss over the stones. Partly fill the center of the pan with water.

To keep the frogs from jumping out, take a piece of window screen and bend it around the pan so that it fits tightly. Fasten the two ends together with wire. Around the top of the screen make five or six 3-inch cuts and bend the screen inward, leaving a space in the center where you can drop some food. If the screen is not bent inward, the frogs can climb up and take off from the top. This kind of frog pond may be kept indoors, or on a porch, or outside in a yard.

WHAT TO FEED

Give newly hatched tadpoles green water or green pond scum, if any is available. If not, try a piece of parboiled or raw lettuce or spinach, or tiny bits of hard-boiled egg yolk. Always keep growing plants in the aquarium; the tadpoles will eat the algae which forms on the plant leaves and on the glass sides. Larger tadpoles like a bit of raw beef or liver or fish once in a while; they may also eat prepared fish food.

Frogs eat earthworms, water worms, meal worms, flies and other land insects, water insects, small fishes, bits of raw meat, and raw fish, also tadpoles and smaller frogs.

HOW TO FEED

A tadpole has a small mouth and horny jaws with which it can scrape up its food. In an aquarium a tadpole will clean the algae off the glass and bottom; it will eat fish food that falls to the bottom; and it will nibble at plant leaves and bits of raw meat and fish.

A frog has a large mouth which can open wide to take in a surprisingly large portion of food. Bullfrogs may eat other frogs only a little smaller than themselves. Never put a large and a small frog together.

Frogs catch their food both on land and in water. The frog's tongue is fastened to the front of its mouth instead of to its throat. To catch a flying insect, the frog shoots its tongue out so fast that you, and the insect, can hardly see it.

Put live food into the frog aquarium whenever it is available. Raw meat or fish may be given once every day or two, although a frog can go without feeding for a longer time if necessary. Put the bit of meat or fish on the end of a broomstraw or toothpick and dangle it in front of the frog. If the frog is hungry, the food will disappear quickly.

In winter, out of doors, frogs dig into the mud and hibernate. In a warm room they will not hibernate, but they become inactive and lose their appetites. Offer them some food every few days so that they can eat if they want to. By February or March they should begin to eat more and become more lively.

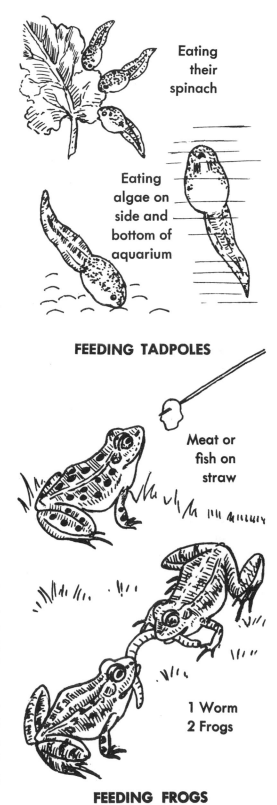

Eating their spinach

Eating algae on side and bottom of aquarium

FEEDING TADPOLES

Meat or fish on straw

1 Worm 2 Frogs

FEEDING FROGS

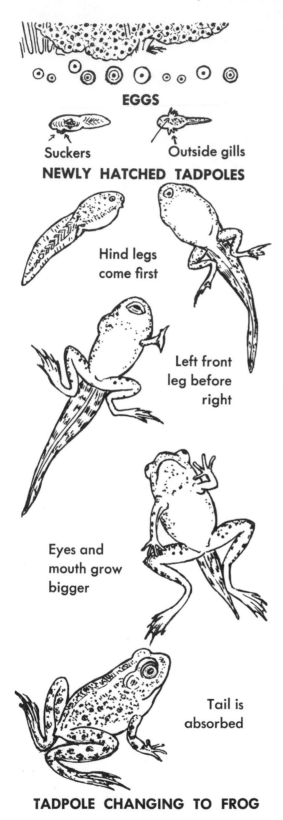

EGGS

Suckers

Outside gills

NEWLY HATCHED TADPOLES

Hind legs
come first

Left front
leg before
right

Eyes and
mouth grow
bigger

Tail is
absorbed

TADPOLE CHANGING TO FROG

LIFE HISTORY

In spring frogs awaken from their winter sleep. Now they are ready to mate and lay eggs. From ponds, lakes, and pools you can hear the croaking chorus of the male frogs. Soon they are joined by the females, who start to lay their eggs. Frog eggs look like dark dots in a jelly coating. Some kinds float in masses on the surface; some are attached to plant stems or leaves.

After a few days to two or three weeks, depending on the kind of frog and the temperature of the water, the eggs hatch into tiny tadpoles. For the first few days the tadpoles cling to something in the water with suckers under their heads. Their mouths are not open. They have outside gills on each side of the head. Soon their mouths open and they swim about. A fold of skin grows over the gills leaving a breathing hole in the left side. The tadpole breathes water in through nostrils and mouth and lets it out through the breathing hole.

Sometime in summer (the second one for green frogs, and the second or third for bullfrogs) the tadpole begins to change into a frog. The hind legs come through first. Later the left front leg comes out through the breathing hole; the right leg breaks through the skin soon after. The small mouth begins to widen; the eyes grow larger and more prominent. The tadpole keeps opening and closing its mouth to let water flow in and out since the breathing hole is closed by the front leg.

After a few days the gills are replaced by lungs and the tadpole comes to the surface to breathe air. In an aquarium, tadpoles should be given something to rest on out of water as soon as their front legs begin to develop.

Along with the other changes, the tadpole's tail grows shorter. While the tail is being absorbed, it furnishes enough nourishment so that the tadpole does not have to eat. Before the tail is gone, the tadpole sometimes hops on land. After the tail is gone, the tadpole is a frog. Now it swims or hops around looking for insects, worms, small fishes, and other animal food instead of the soft vegetable stuff that tadpoles eat.

Most frogs live in ponds or along the shore. But some frogs, like the tree frogs and the wood frog, live on land just as the toad does.

TOAD, TREE FROGS, WOOD FROG

Although toads, tree frogs, and wood frogs live on land, they lay their eggs in water. The eggs hatch into tadpoles which you can raise in your aquarium. When these tadpoles change into toads or frogs, they should be set free in the woods or kept in a terrarium.

From the middle of April through May TOADS go to ponds to breed. The females lay eggs in long strings of jelly. After four to twelve days the eggs hatch into tiny black tadpoles. In a month or two the tadpoles are about an inch long and black with golden specks. Then they grow legs and change into ½ -inch toads.

Adult toads have a warty light or dark brown skin. The female grows 4½ to 5 inches long, the male about 3½ inches. If you can capture a pair of breeding toads and keep them in a large aquarium or dispan pond (see page 46), the female will lay her eggs while the male fertilizes them. Set the toads free afterward and raise the tadpoles which hatch from the eggs like frog tadpoles.

In April, SPRING PEEPERS lay their eggs singly on underwater plants. The eggs hatch into tadpoles which grow a little over an inch long. The tadpoles have dark purplish blotches on the back and are cream colored underneath. In summer they change into tiny frogs which are brown with a dark X on the back.

Around May TREE FROGS, or TREE TOADS, lay brown and yellow eggs which are attached to plants that live under water or float in small groups. In four or five days the eggs hatch into tiny yellow tadpoles. The tadpoles grow nearly 2 inches long. Then they have reddish-orange tails with black blotches. They change into ½ -inch frogs. The frogs grow nearly 2 inches long and are grayish-green with a dark patch on the back.

In March or April, WOOD FROGS lay their eggs in woodland pools. The eggs are in jelly masses attached to something under water. Soon they float to the surface, take on a greenish color, and look like pond scum. The tadpoles are olive-brown on the back with light lines on the upper jaw, light pinkish or bronze underneath. They grow 2 inches long, then change into frogs a little over ½ inch long. Full-grown frogs, 2 or 3 inches long, are light or dark brown with a dark cheek patch.

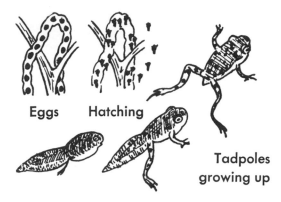

Eggs   Hatching   Tadpoles growing up

AMERICAN TOAD

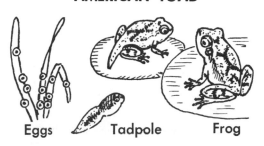

Eggs   Tadpole   Frog

SPRING PEEPER

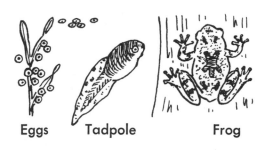

Eggs   Tadpole   Frog

TREE FROG

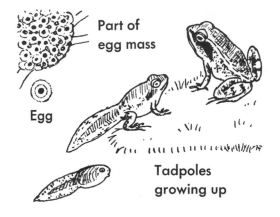

Part of egg mass

Egg   Tadpoles growing up

WOOD FROG

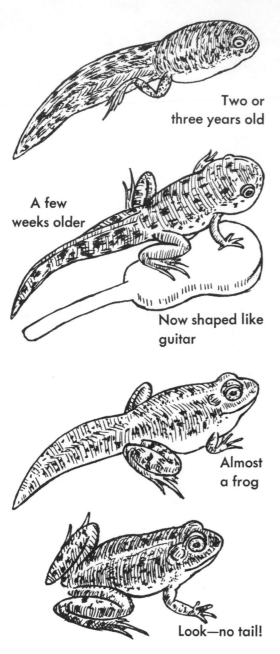

Two or three years old

A few weeks older

Now shaped like guitar

Almost a frog

Look—no tail!

BULLFROG GROWING UP

BULLFROG AND GREEN FROG

BULLFROGS and GREEN FROGS live in or near water most of the time. Bullfrogs come out of hibernation late in spring. In June and July, the males croak in ponds and lakes. The females lay eggs in jelly masses 2 feet and more across which float among the weeds along the shore. In about a week the tadpoles hatch. They do not change into frogs for two or three years. In winter they hibernate in the mud. (Indoors in an aquarium, they remain active.) The tadpoles grow 6 or 7 inches long. They are greenish-brown with black specks on the back and yellow underneath. They change into frogs which are less than 2 inches long. The young frogs are brown tinged with green and spotted with black on the back, and creamy underneath.

When full grown, bullfrogs are 6 to 10 inches long in the body, with very long legs. The male is smaller than the female. He is olive-green with a yellow throat; the female is usually more brownish and spotted. The tadpoles are good aquarium pets; the young frogs are not. They are apt to be shy and not easy to feed.

In May or later the green frog lays its eggs. The eggs float in jelly masses about 12 inches across on the surface of shallow water near shore. In a week or less the eggs hatch. The tadpoles grow about 2½ inches long and are olive-green speckled with dark brown. In their second summer they change into inch-long frogs. The young frogs are olive-brown or greenish with black specks on the back, bright green on the cheeks, and light underneath. Full-grown frogs are 4 or 5 inches long, brownish with some dark markings on the back, bright green on the head and shoulders, and white with black marks underneath. The tadpoles should be in an aquarium, and the young frogs may be kept in a tank which has a wet and dry area.

First summer

Second summer

Young Frog

GREEN FROG GROWING UP

MEADOW FROGS

LEOPARD and PICKEREL FROGS live in ponds and lakes in spring. In summer they often hop about in moist, or sometimes dry, meadows looking for insects to eat.

Leopard frogs are green or brownish on the back with rounded dark spots bordered by white. The fold of skin running down each side is yellow or bronze; the underside is white. These frogs grow to be 3 or 4 inches long. They are among the first to come out of hibernation. Early in March the males call in the ponds with a hoarse croak.

The females lay eggs in jelly masses 3 to 6 inches across. The masses are usually fastened to plants in shallow water. They appear dark because the eggs are close together. It takes from four to twenty days for the eggs to hatch into tiny black tadpoles. The tadpoles grow for two or three months until they are about 3 inches long. Then they are a dark olive-brown speckled with black on the back, reddish under the chin, and light underneath.

In July and August the tadpoles change into frogs an inch or less long. The little frogs are alert. They have black polka dots on their green backs and brown sides. Since they are usually tame and easily fed, they may be kept as pets until they grow too large. Keep them in a container that has as much land as water.

Pickerel frogs are usually more brownish or more bronze than leopard frogs. Their black spots are more square than round. They have a bright orange patch under their hind legs which is lacking in leopard frogs. The males grow to be 2½ inches and the females over 3 inches long.

In April the males begin to call in shallow ponds. Their call is a grunting croak that sounds like snoring. During May the females lay their eggs in rounded masses of jelly about 2 inches across. The masses are either floating or attached to plants in shallow water. In warm water the eggs may hatch in four days; in cool water it may take nineteen days. The tadpoles grow to be 3 inches long. They are greenish-brown with black specks on the back, have purplish tail crests, and are light underneath.

During August the tadpoles change into slender, delicate little frogs. Young pickerel frogs are more shy and are harder to raise in captivity than leopard frogs.

About 2½ months old

3 months

4 months

LEOPARD FROG GROWING UP

LEOPARD FROG

PICKEREL FROG

SALAMANDERS

Water-living salamanders make odd and interesting pets for the aquarium. You can catch full-grown salamanders or, by finding eggs, you can watch larvae hatch and grow.

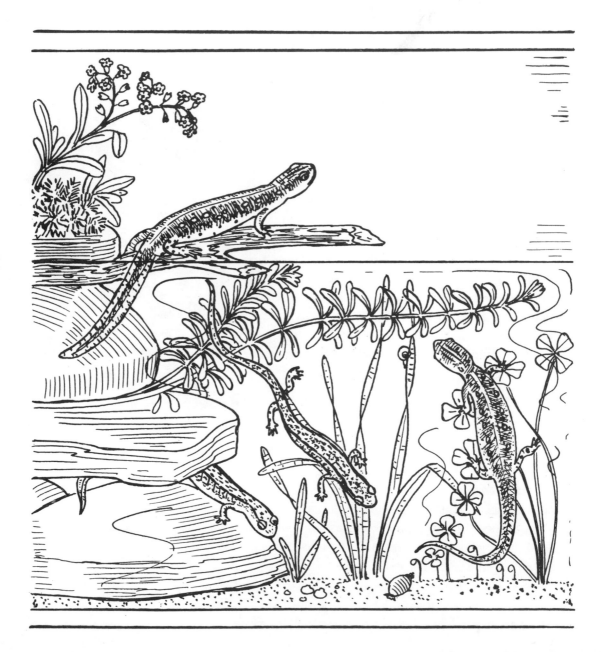

Salamanders may be kept in a container which has a land and water area.

WHERE TO FIND

Look for salamander eggs in spring in shallow water among water plants. Look for larval salamanders in late spring and summer in ponds, streams, springs, swamps, and lakes. Adult salamanders you may find in or near water, sometimes under stones, leaves, or logs. Some kinds are more active at night.

HOW TO CATCH

Scoop eggs up carefully in any convenient container. Catch larval salamanders in a small net, sieve, can, measuring cup, or other utensil. Catch adults in the same way, or by hand if you can. Try to keep in front of the salamander when catching it. Do not grab it by the tail because it breaks off easily. Salamanders are not poisonous to handle, but they are slippery and hard to hold.

HOW TO CARRY

Carry salamander eggs or larval salamanders in a jar, can, or pail with pond water. Carry adults in a container with a small amount of water. Securely cover the container with netting or a lid with holes punched in it. Do not let the container become overheated.

HOW TO KEEP

Salamander eggs may be kept in an aquarium with shallow pond water. Out of doors they hatch in from two to ten weeks; indoors they may hatch sooner. You can watch the dark larvae developing inside the eggs.

The larvae may be kept in an aquarium with shallow water, algae, and other plants. They breathe oxygen in the water. Change the water when necessary, using pond or aerated tap water and keep the water cool. Do not put too many larvae into one container. Do not put them with adult salamanders, frogs, or other meat-eating creatures.

Net

Strainer

Large cup

Hand

HOW TO CATCH

Butter dish

Flower pot

Stone islands

Aquarium with island

HOW TO KEEP

Broomstraw

Toothpick in hollow straw

FEEDING STICKS

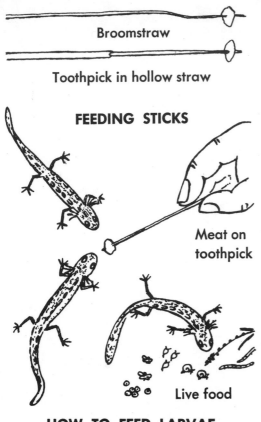

Meat on toothpick

Live food

HOW TO FEED LARVAE

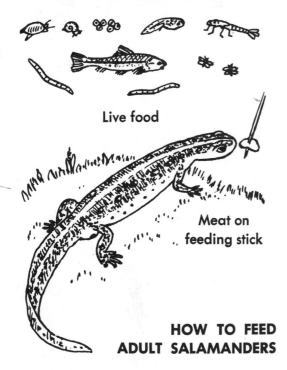

Live food

Meat on feeding stick

HOW TO FEED ADULT SALAMANDERS

Adult salamanders and adult larvae about to change should be kept in an aquarium which has some kind of a dry island in the water. The island may be a flowerpot or dish filled with soil and growing plants, or a pile of stones. Most salamanders are able to climb, so cover their aquarium securely with a screen. Keep the aquarium in a partly sunny, but not hot, place. Have enough shade so the salamanders can take shelter.

WHAT TO FEED

Salamanders, both larvae and adults, eat animal food.

The larvae eat water insects, water fleas (daphnia) and other small crustaceans, aphids and other small land insects, small snails, and worms. In captivity they will also eat tiny bits of raw meat and fish, fish roe, bits of hard-boiled egg yolk, cottage cheese, and prepared fish food.

Adult salamanders eat snails, worms, small tadpoles, small fishes, fish eggs, insects, and other small creatures. In captivity they will eat small earthworms; white worms; raw fish or meat; and sometimes cooked egg yolk, cottage cheese, or fish food.

HOW TO FEED

Drop food into the water or put it on the land area. Meat and other non-living food should be removed if not eaten within a few hours. Salamanders are usually most interested in food that moves. Try putting bits of meat, fish, or other food on the end of a straw or stick and wiggling it slowly in front of them. If hungry, they will creep up, grab the food in their jaws, and pull it off with a jerk of the head.

Feed salamanders as much as they will eat at one time every day or two. They will usually not eat more than three or four mouthfuls. If necessary, they can go without food for several days. Notice whether they are more active during the day or evening and feed them at that time. Notice also whether they take the food more readily in water or on land.

In winter salamanders are usually inactive and, therefore, eat very little during the winter months.

LIFE HISTORY

Male and female salamanders collect in ponds or other bodies of water in spring (sometimes in summer or fall) to mate and lay eggs. The males deposit spermatophores, like little cones of jelly, which are picked up by the females. The females then lay eggs which are jelly coated like frog eggs. The eggs either float in masses near the surface, or are attached singly to plants, stones, or other supports in the water. A few kinds of salamanders lay eggs on land in logs or under stones or leaves. Some salamanders may lay eggs in a large aquarium.

Eggs laid in water hatch into larvae which look like slender tadpoles with a fringe of gills on each side of the head. Some have legs, some develop legs as they grow. The external gills remain until the larvae are ready to change into adults. The larvae breathe oxygen in the water; adults, except those that have gills, breathe air.

Most larvae change into adults in late summer or fall. In winter some salamanders hibernate, but some remain active even in ice-covered streams.

TWO-LINED SALAMANDER

This salamander lives among rocks at the edge of a stream. It grows about 4 inches long. It is grayish-brown with black specks on the back, has a dark stripe down each side, and is yellowish underneath. It is quick moving and hard to catch.

In spring or early summer the female lays eggs on the underside of rocks in water. The eggs hatch in about ten weeks into ¼-inch, legless larvae. In two weeks the larvae have four legs and are brown with a row of black and white spots along each side. By the end of their first or second summer they are 2 inches long and ready to change into adults.

A few larvae may be kept in a small aquarium with shallow water. Adult two-lined salamanders may be kept in an aquarium with shallow water. Have some stones and earth with grass or moss in the aquarium. The salamanders' aquarium should be securely covered with a tight screen (removable for feeding), because they are able to climb and slither through very small openings.

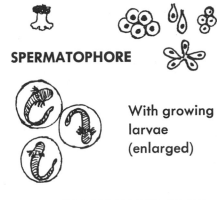

SPERMATOPHORE

With growing larvae (enlarged)

SALAMANDER EGGS

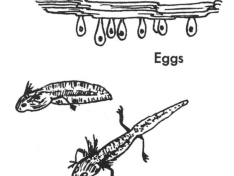

Eggs

Larvae

TWO-LINED SALAMANDER

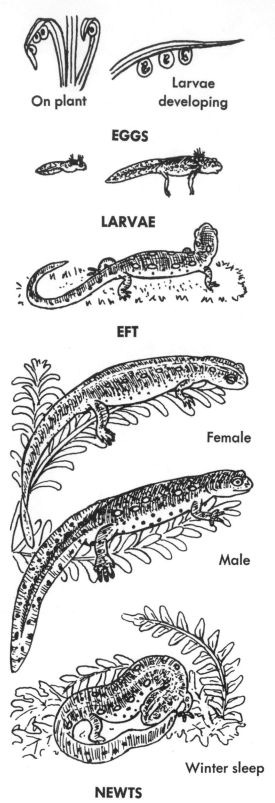

On plant

Larvae developing

EGGS

LARVAE

EFT

Female

Male

Winter sleep

NEWTS

NEWT

Newts are common in many ponds and quiet streams. They are slow moving and fairly easy to catch. They make hardy and interesting aquarium pets.

Adult newts are 3 to 5 inches long. They are greenish-brown with black specks and red spots on the back, and yellow underneath. The male is darker than the female and has larger red spots. He also has larger hind legs and feet with which he grasps the female around the neck during the courtship dance. This may take place during fall or spring.

In spring the female lays eggs on the leaves of water plants near the surface. She rolls the leaves over to conceal the eggs. Out of doors the eggs hatch in three to six weeks, indoors in less time. The larvae are greenish-brown with reddish gills. They are ½ inch long at first, and have a tail fin but no legs. By fall they have legs and are about 2½ inches long. Soon they lose their gills and tail fin and change into small red salamanders, which are called efts. The efts live on land for a year or two. Then they return to the water and change again, this time into newts. Sometimes the eft stage is skipped; sometimes it lasts for years. Red efts should not be kept in an aquarium. They should be placed in a container with earth and plants on the bottom and a dish of water.

Adult newts should be kept in an aquarium with water enough for swimming and an island to rest on. Have some growing plants on the island, because newts like to climb on them. In the water the newts often come to the surface to belch an air bubble since they breathe air.

Newts are easy to tame and raise. They will usually eat bits of raw meat on the end of a straw soon after they are captured. They eat either day or night, in or out of water. A male and female may be kept together, but two males are likely to fight.

Like other salamanders, newts often shed their skin. They pull it off over their head and eat it afterward.

In winter newts are less active; sometimes they curl up on moist land and sleep for days at a time. They eat very little but should be offered food when they move around. By February or March they are usually active and hungry again.

LARGE SALAMANDERS

The TIGER SALAMANDER is black with yellowish markings and slimy. It grows 7 or even 10 inches in length. It usually lives on soft ground, but early in spring it goes to ponds to breed. The female lays eggs in jelly masses attached to plants in shallow water. In three or four weeks the eggs hatch into ½-inch greenish larvae without legs. By the end of summer the larvae have legs and are usually full grown. They may change to adults then or the following spring. In some parts of the western United States, these salamanders retain their gills and remain water creatures all their lives. These are called axolotls. Captive larvae and axolotls should be kept in an aquarium. Captive tiger salamanders need a moist terrarium.

The SPOTTED SALAMANDER is black on the back with round, yellow spots. It is stout-bodied, broad-headed, and grows 6 to 9 inches long. In early spring spotted salamanders collect in ponds to breed. The eggs are in masses attached to water plants. In two to four weeks they hatch into greenish-brown larvae ½ inch long with stubs of front legs and feathery gills. The larvae soon grow legs. In three months they are about 3 inches long and ready to change into adult salamanders. The larvae may be kept in an aquarium, the adults in a terrarium.

The MUD PUPPY grows to be a foot or more long. It is brown with black spots and has red gills which look like wavy ears. It lives in water, usually at the bottom of slow streams and ponds among plants. In spring the female lays her eggs on the underside of stones or other support. The eggs hatch after six to nine weeks into ¾-inch, legless larvae. They are dark with a yellow stripe down each side. The larvae soon grow short legs, but it takes them seven or eight years to become adult mud puppies. They may live twenty years. Captive mud puppies need a large aquarium with cool aerated water.

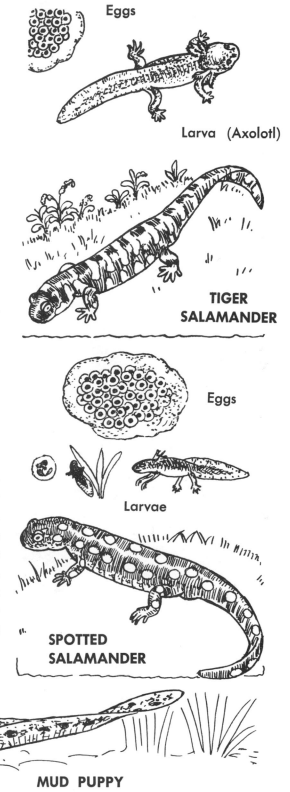

Eggs

Larva (Axolotl)

TIGER SALAMANDER

Eggs

Larvae

SPOTTED SALAMANDER

MUD PUPPY

TURTLES

Whether you buy your turtle or go out and capture a wild one for your aquarium, you will find that it makes an appealing, easy-to-care-for member of your pet collection.

KINDS OF TURTLES

Some turtles live mostly in water, some in fields and woods. Naturally only water-living turtles should be kept in an aquarium, and these should have some means of resting out of water.

This turtle can scratch

WHERE TO FIND

Look for turtles in and around ponds and slow streams. You may see them swimming in the water, sunning themselves on logs or rocks, or crawling along the banks. Unless you have a very large aquarium or an outdoor pool, only small turtles should be taken home for pets.

This turtle would like to scratch, but cannot

HOW TO CATCH AND CARRY

Use a strong net to catch a turtle in the water. At the water's edge you may be able to pick one up by hand, especially if it is young.

If you hold the turtle upside down by the back of its shell, it will not be able to bite or kick you. Be careful not to drop it. A cracked shell can be fatal.

Carry the turtle home in a pail, a can with holes in the lid, a box with air holes in the cover, or a strong bag. It is not necessary to have water.

Lasso for small snapping turtle

HOW TO HOLD

Bulb bowl for baby turtles

HOW TO KEEP

For baby turtles a large bulb bowl with incurved sides is useful because the turtles can't climb up the sides. A piece of sod or moss may be used for an island in the middle.

Small turtles may be kept in a glass aquarium. A piece of wood shingle fastened to one side at the water's surface, a large flat stone, or a pile of small stones rising above the water will give the turtles a place to rest out of water.

Larger turtles may be kept in a wash basin or dish pan partly filled with water. A pile of stones covered with moss or grass will make an island in the middle. A piece of wire screening may be cut as described on page 46 and placed around the pan to keep the turtles from crawling out and wandering off on their own.

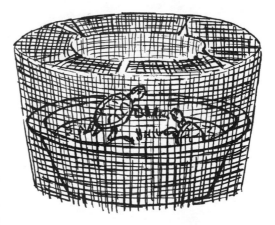

Dishpan for larger turtles

Horny jaws instead of teeth

Feeding from fingers

Stalking

Grabbing

Looking for more

FEEDING

WHAT TO FEED

Most turtles eat both animal and plant food. Out of doors they eat fishes and fish eggs, worms, snails, slugs, insects and their larvae, tadpoles, crayfish, and other small creatures, as well as grasses, moss, algae, seeds, and other plant material.

In captivity turtles will eat their natural food. They will also eat bits of raw meat such as chopped beef and liver, pieces of raw fish, earthworms and other small worms, small shell creatures, and lettuce, slices of vegetables and fruits. These foods are better than the prepared food and ant "eggs" sold in pet shops; in fact no turtle can live for long on the prepared foods.

HOW TO FEED

Feed medium-sized turtles about once every other day. Give them as much as they will eat at one time, about six pieces of meat or fish, or several worms. Baby turtles may be fed the same food in smaller amounts once a day. Pieces of lettuce or other vegetables may be left in the aquarium until they start to spoil. Moss and grass for the turtles to nibble on may be grown on a pile of stones rising above the water.

Turtles do not have teeth, but the edge of their jaws is horny and sharp enough to tear food apart. Some kinds of turtles have a down-turned beak on the upper jaw. Turtles use their claws to push and pull their food apart, but they do not push their food into their mouths with their feet. Tame turtles will soon learn to eat from their owner's fingers.

A water-living turtle usually prefers to eat under water. If its food is dropped into the water, the turtle will creep up and grab it in its mouth.

In order to keep the aquarium clean, turtles may be removed for feeding. They can be put into a sink or large pan that is partly filled with water.

In winter captive turtles may become sluggish and less hungry, but if they are kept in a warm room, they are more likely to remain active. They should still be offered food at regular intervals.

LIFE HISTORY

Baby turtles hatch from eggs laid in spring or summer. With her hind legs, the female digs a hole in sand or soft earth; or sometimes she makes a hole in a hollow log. In the hole she lays five to eight or more eggs, each an inch long. The eggs are light colored, oval or round, and soft or hard shelled depending on the kind of turtle. After laying, the turtle covers the eggs with sand or other material and leaves them. Toward the end of summer they hatch into tiny turtles which look like small editions of the adults.

Although they may hatch some distance from the shore, the young turtles are able to find their way to the water. There they can swim about and find their food.

It usually takes four to six years or longer for turtles to become mature. They may live for twenty-five years or longer.

In winter most water-living turtles hibernate in the mud, but some may swim about a little even in an ice-covered pond.

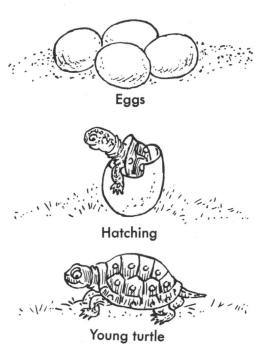

Eggs

Hatching

Young turtle

LIFE HISTORY

PARTS OF A TURTLE

A turtle's body is covered by an upper shell (carapace) and a lower shell (plastron). The upper shell has wide ribs on the inside and large scales grown together on the outside. The shell is so thick and strong that it gives protection from most enemies.

Turtles have good eyesight and a keen sense of smell both under water and in the air. They breathe air, but can hold enough in their lungs to stay under water for a long time. The skin of the throat throbs back and forth to help force air into the lungs.

Snapping turtle's beak

Spotted turtle no beak—no bite

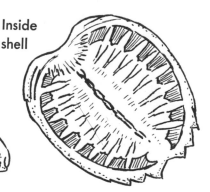

Inside shell

CARAPACE

PLASTRON

PARTS OF A TURTLE

PAINTED TURTLES

SPOTTED TURTLES

POND TURTLES

The PAINTED TURTLE looks a bit like a clown with its wide white or yellow mouth and red-striped neck and legs. Its upper shell, which grows to 7 inches long, is shiny olive-brown or black with yellow lines between the scales and red markings around the border. The male has long, thin nails on his front feet. The female has stubby ones. The tail of the male is longer than that of the female. When the female is four years old or older, she begins to lay eggs. In June or July she digs a hole in the ground near a body of water and lays from six to twelve white or pinkish oval eggs. Late in summer the eggs hatch into inch-long turtles.

Look for little painted turtles for your aquarium among plants and green scum at the edge of a pond or on rocks or logs in the water. The young turtles quickly become tame and make amusing pets. They have a funny, babyish expression on their little painted faces and a lively way of crawling and tumbling around.

A larger painted turtle is best kept in an aquarium by itself because it is likely to annoy other creatures, although it does not bite people. Painted turtles eat meat and plant food, which they swallow under water.

The SPOTTED TURTLE has a smooth black upper shell with many yellow polka dots, which also appear on its feet and head, Its feet are only partly webbed because it does not live in water all the time. The male turtle grows 5 inches long, the female, 4 inches. He has a longer tail and brown eyes; her eyes are orange and the horny part of her jaw is yellow. Late in June she digs a hole in a sandy place near a body of water and lays two to four oval white eggs. In September the eggs hatch into small turtles which have only one yellow spot on each scale.

Look for spotted turtles in brooks and ponds, and possibly in the woods near water. When approached, they are apt to take off slowly and swim to the bottom, where they hide under mud or plants. After they are captured, they are gentle and do not bite. They soon learn to take food (meat or fish) from one's fingers; they grab the food in their mouths and duck under water to swallow it. When food is dropped into the water, the turtles search around until they find it.

MUSK, MUD AND SNAPPING TURTLES

Musk and mud turtles grow 4 or 5 inches long. They live on the muddy bottoms of ponds and sluggish streams.

The adult MUSK TURTLE has a smooth, brown, arched upper shell and a small, yellowish under shell which can bend a little at each end. Its head has a slender snout and two yellow stripes, one above and one below the eye. It can snap and bite if annoyed. The male's tail is longer than the female's and has a blunt nail at the tip. Musk glands near the base of the hind legs give off a bad odor. This turtle often buries itself in the mud. It can stay under water a long time, weeks if necessary.

Baby musk turtles a little over an inch long are not vicious or smelly and so make better pets than adults. Instead of being smooth, their shell is rough with a saw-tooth edge. They have the two yellow lines on each side of the head like the adults. They may be kept in an aquarium with a land and water area and fed meat food.

The MUD TURTLE resembles the musk turtle, but it does not have distinct yellow stripes on the head and it has a larger under shell. The under shell is hinged at both ends so that it can be drawn up tight against the upper shell to enclose the turtle's body like a box. This turtle is more gentle than the musk turtle, but it is harder to find because it is not common anywhere.

Adult SNAPPING TURTLES are large, vicious, and not suitable for pets. Baby snapping turtles, under 3 inches long, make fairly good pets. They may be kept in an aquarium with a land and water area. If the aquarium doesn't have high sides, keep a screen over the top because the turtles are strong and active. They are able to climb, using their long tail as a sort of fifth leg.

A young snapping turtle has a rough, brown, upper shell with three ridges along the back and a saw-toothed edge at the back end. It has webbed feet and a long tail which is ridged on top. Its under shell is small. This permits it to move around easily. When the turtle is laid on its back, it looks like a baby (not a very handsome one) in its cradle.

Feed snapping turtles meat food, but not with the fingers, because they can bite. They swallow their food under water.

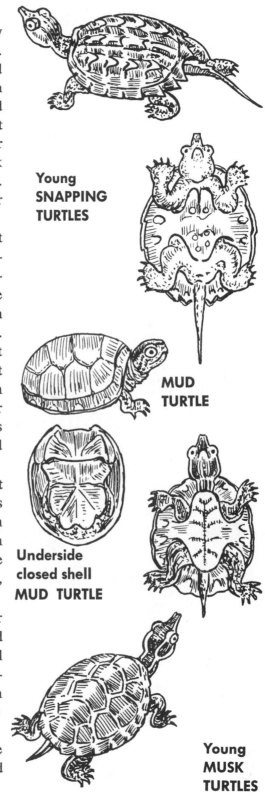

Young
SNAPPING
TURTLES

MUD
TURTLE

Underside
closed shell
MUD TURTLE

Young
MUSK
TURTLES

CRAYFISHES

A crayfish may be kept in an aquarium that has been partly filled with water. The crayfish in the picture is about to catch the minnows that have been put in for it to eat.

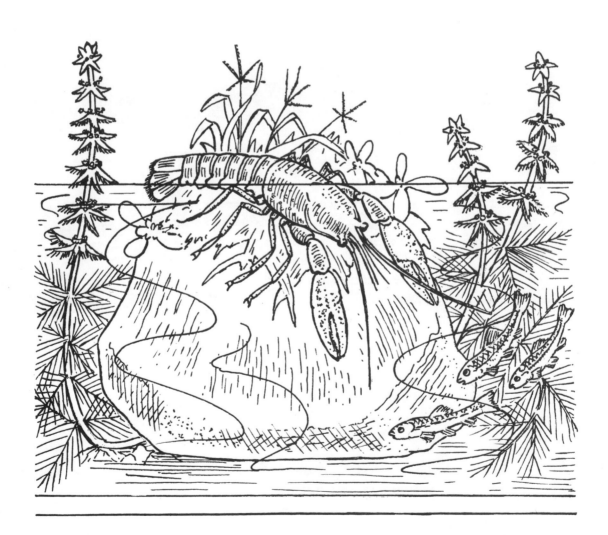

A crayfish has a hard shell which is divided into segments. It has ten legs, eight to walk on and two in front that are enlarged into claws. Crayfishes grow 3 to 5 inches long. They are grayish or brownish, sometimes tinged with red. They live along the edges of ponds and slow streams, where they hide under rocks or in holes.

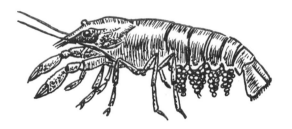

**Female with eggs
glued to her swimmerets**

HOW TO CATCH AND CARRY

Use a strong net, a sieve, or your hands, to catch a crayfish. Hold it by the middle of the back so that it will not nip you. As crayfishes are active at night, you can sometimes find them with a flashlight.

Carry each crayfish in its own container. This may be a pail, box, can, or something similar. Crayfishes need air, but can do without water for a time.

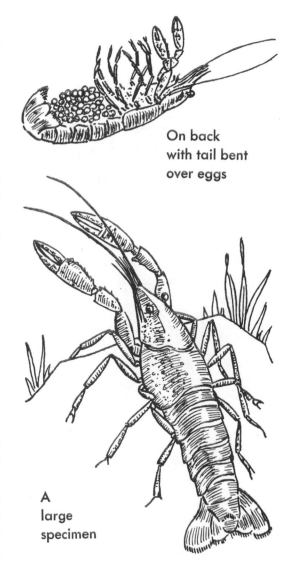

**On back
with tail bent
over eggs**

HOW TO KEEP AND FEED

To avoid fights, keep only one crayfish in an aquarium. A glass tank, dish pan, or other container may be used; have a screen over the top if the sides are not high. Have the water about three inches deep with a stone or sod island in the middle. Change the water often to keep it clean.

Out of doors, crayfishes eat minnows, water insects, and other small animal life, which they catch in their claws. They also eat dead animal food, and living and dead plants. In an aquarium they eat bits of raw meat and fish, earthworms, insects, coarse fish food, and plants. Drop food into the water about every other day.

LIFE HISTORY

Crayfishes mate in spring or throughout the year. The female carries her eggs glued to the swimmerets under the tail end of her body. She waves the eggs back and forth in the water to aerate them. In about two months the eggs hatch into tiny crayfish. The young cling to the mother's swimmerets for about a week, then they drop off and care for themselves. Most crayfishes live less than two years, but some kinds may live several years.

**A
large
specimen**

CRAYFISHES

INSECTS

Water insects make fascinating and unusual aquarium inhabitants, though many people fail to think of them as pets. They are easy to find and catch—also easy to raise.

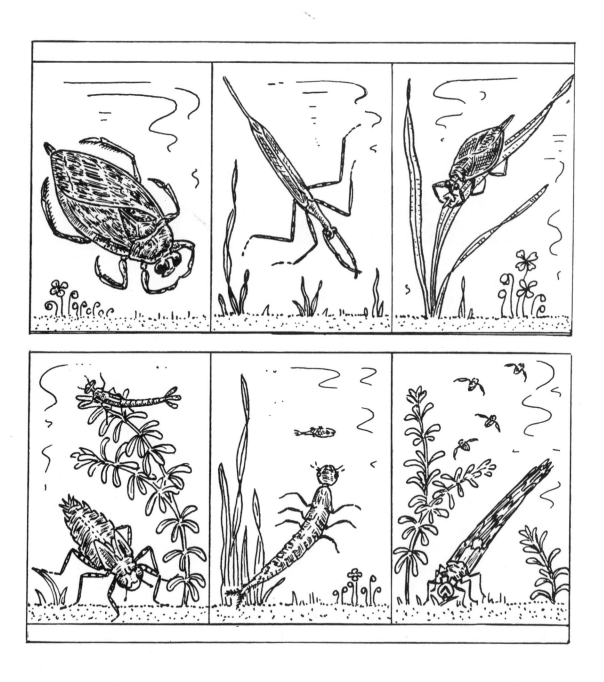

WHERE TO FIND

Water insects make odd and interesting aquarium pets. Many kinds are easy to find, catch, and raise. Look for them along the shallow edge of ponds, lakes, and streams, among water plants, in pond scum, under stones, and in the bottom mud.

HOW TO CATCH AND CARRY

To catch insects that collect at the surface, use a cloth or wire net on a long handle. Draw the net through the water and scoop up a group of insects before they have a chance to scatter if possible. Where there are water plants, work the net around the stems and leaves. You may also find insects by turning over and examining the leaves.

To find insects on the bottom of a pond or stream, use a kitchen strainer on a long handle, a hardware cloth scoop or, in shallow water, a rubber scoop (from the kitchen sink), and a kitchen strainer. Take up a little mud and let it drain; pick out any bits of life with a spoon or tweezers, since fingers might get bitten.

To catch insects in flowing streams, a wire-screen seine may be held across the stream.

Carry your catch home in a net-covered container partly filled with water such as a jar, can, or pail. Put only one kind of insect into a container.

Keep insects in any of the aquariums shown on pages 10 and 11. If the insects can climb or fly, cover the aquarium with a net or screen. Change the water when it starts to become cloudy. Do not keep large and small meat-eating insects in one aquarium because the large ones would probably eat the smaller ones.

Out of doors meat-eating insects eat smaller insects, crustaceans, snails, worms, small fishes, fish eggs, small tadpoles, and other small creatures. Plant-eating insects eat water plants including algae.

In captivity insects will eat the same food as they do out of doors. The meat-eaters will also eat bits of raw meat and fish. Put the meat or fish on the end of a toothpick or broomstraw and wiggle it as moving food is more likely to be noticed.

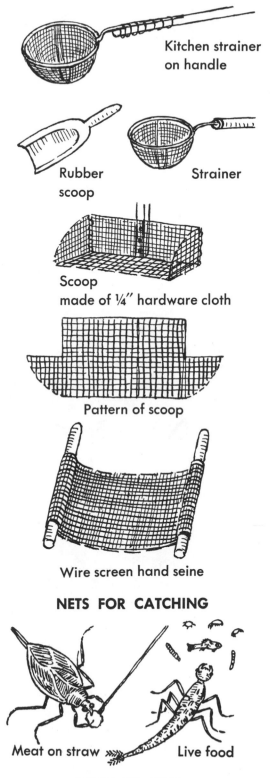

Kitchen strainer on handle

Rubber scoop

Strainer

Scoop made of ¼″ hardware cloth

Pattern of scoop

Wire screen hand seine

NETS FOR CATCHING

Meat on straw

Live food

HOW TO FEED

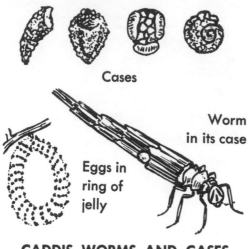

Cases

Worm
in its case

Eggs in
ring of
jelly

CADDIS WORMS AND CASES

CADDIS WORMS

In streams and ponds, on rocks, water plants, and on the bottom, you may find cases, or tubes, of caddis worms. The cases, from ½ to 2 inches long, are made of tiny pebbles, shells, bits of bark, stems, or leaves of water plants fastened together with glue-like saliva. The worms live in their cases. Only the front part of their body comes out when they move around. They breathe under water through gills or, in some kinds, through the thin body skin. Most caddis worms eat plants, including algae. Some take meat food.

Keep caddis worms in an aquarium with a few inches of pond water, some water plants, and sand. Add other materials, such as colored beads and tiny shells, and watch the worms add to their cases. The worm in the picture is yellow and black; it has a case of bark and leaves.

Caddis worms hatch from eggs laid in water by caddis flies. When the worms are full grown, they withdraw into their cases, form pupae, and change into caddis flies.

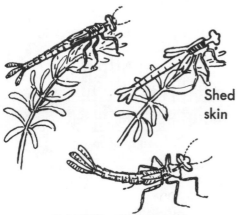

Shed
skin

DAMSEL FLY NYMPHS

DRAGONFLY AND DAMSEL FLY NYMPHS

These nymphs hatch from eggs laid by dragon and damsel flies in water, usually on plants. They live in ponds or brooks, in the bottom mud or on plants. DRAGONFLY NYMPHS grow to be ½ or 1½ inches long. They are brown or greenish with hard-skinned, rather stout bodies which may be smooth or fuzzy. They breathe oxygen in the water by passing it in and out of their tail end. They also shoot themselves forward by squirting out water.

DAMSEL FLY NYMPHS are small, delicate, and brownish or bright green like the water plants among which they live. They breathe through three flat gills at the tail end.

Both kinds of nymphs are meat-eating; they feed on insects and other tiny creatures. They catch their prey by thrusting out their long, hinged underlip. Some nymphs change into dragon or damsel flies the first summer or fall, some live as nymphs through the winter. In an aquarium keep the nymphs in shallow water. Have growing plants or sticks reaching above the water. When they are grown, the nymphs climb above water, split their skins down the back, and emerge as winged creatures.

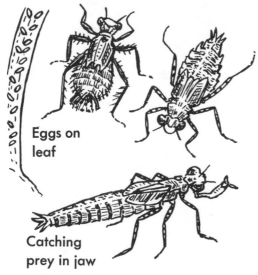

Eggs on
leaf

Catching
prey in jaw

DRAGONFLY NYMPHS

WATER BEETLES

These beetles live in water most of the time although they have wings and can fly. They lay eggs in water, usually on plants. The eggs hatch into grub-like larvae. Full-grown larvae crawl out on moist earth, form pupae, and change into beetles.

WHIRLIGIG BEETLES are small, black or bronze beetles which whirl on the surface or dive under water. They sometimes squeak by rubbing their wings against their bodies. The larvae are pale and slender and have a row of fringed gills on each side. Late in summer they form pupae inside cocoons and, after a few weeks, change into beetles. The beetles live through the winter. They may be kept in a wide-mouthed, covered aquarium. Both larvae and adults eat small insects and other meat food.

The several kinds of DIVING BEETLES are shiny black or brown with threadlike antennae, or feelers. They vary from ¼ to more than 1½ inches in length. To breathe, they hang head down and stick their tail end above the surface. When they dive, they carry a bubble of air under their wings. They swim by using their flat hind legs as oars.

Diving beetle larvae are called WATER TIGERS because of their fierce habits. They catch even creatures that are larger than themselves in their strong jaws. After sucking the juices from their prey, they discard the skins. If handled, they may bite.

Some water tigers grow 2½ inches long. To breathe, they float near the surface with their tail end up. Keep one water tiger in an aquarium by itself. Several diving beetles may be kept together but not with other creatures. Feed water tigers and beetles living animal food or raw meat.

WATER SCAVENGER BEETLES look much like diving beetles, but they can be identified by their club-shaped antennae. They breathe by sticking their antennae above the surface and pulling down a bubble of air.

Female scavenger beetles lay eggs in silken cocoons. The cocoons are either fastened under a leaf, floating, or carried under the beetle's body. The larvae prey on other water creatures. In an aquarium the larvae eat meat food; the adult beetles eat algae, water weed and other plants, decaying material, and meat food.

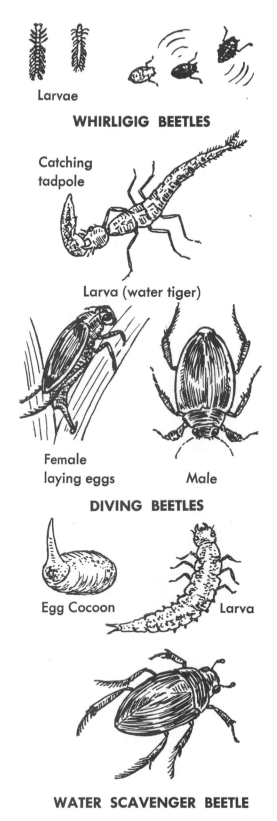

Larvae

WHIRLIGIG BEETLES

Catching tadpole

Larva (water tiger)

Female laying eggs   Male

DIVING BEETLES

Egg Cocoon   Larva

WATER SCAVENGER BEETLE

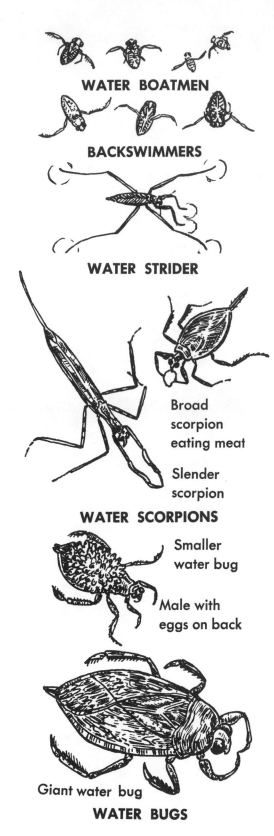

WATER BOATMEN

BACKSWIMMERS

WATER STRIDER

Broad
scorpion
eating meat

Slender
scorpion

WATER SCORPIONS

Smaller
water bug

Male with
eggs on back

Giant water bug

WATER BUGS

WATER BUGS

These bugs lay eggs in the water, usually on plants. Nymphs which hatch from the eggs are shaped like the adults but lack wings. As they grow and molt, wings develop.

All of them, except the boatmen, are meat-eaters. They catch their prey in their clawlike front legs and suck the juices out through their beaklike mouths. Water bugs breathe air, some through tubes at their tail end, and some through a bubble surrounding their body. Most of them can fly and should be kept in a covered container.

WATER BOATMEN and BACKSWIMMERS are ¼ to ½ inch long. They use their long, flattened hind legs like oars. Backswimmers swim upside down, boatmen right-side up. Backswimmers eat small crustaceans and insects, which they paralyze with their poisonous bite. They can also give people a stinging bite. Boatmen are plant-eaters; they scrape up algae with their front legs.

WATER STRIDERS live on the surface, where their feet make dimples but do not sink in. One large kind has a slender body ½ inch long; another small kind has a broad body ¼ inch long; some kinds do not have wings. Striders eat small insects and, in an aquarium, bits of meat. Keep them in a deep container with shallow water.

The SLENDER WATER SCORPION grows 2½ inches long; the BROAD SCORPION, ½ inch long. Both kinds have long breathing tubes at the end of the body which they stick up to the surface for air. They eat live meat food or, in an aquarium, bits of meat from the end of a straw. Keep the small broad scorpion in a container with shallow water and some leaves to hide under. The slender scorpion may be kept in deeper water among growing plants.

GIANT WATER BUGS grow as long as 2 inches. They can fly and are sometimes seen around electric lights. In the water they crawl on the bottom looking for dragonfly nymphs, small fish, and other creatures to eat. They can bite hard, so handle them with care, if at all.

The SMALL WATER BUG grows about 1 inch long. Sometimes one is found with its back covered with eggs. This is the male! The female glues her eggs to his back and he carries them around until they hatch. Both water bugs breathe through short air tubes at the tail end.

INDEX

MORE TO READ

AQUARIUMS

Aquariums, by Anthony Evans (Dover)
Guide to Higher Aquarium Animals, by Edward T. Boardman
  (Cranbrook Institute of Science)
Wonders of the Aquarium, by Sigmund A. Lavine (Dodd Mead)

FISHES

Fisherman's Encyclopedia, edited by Ira N. Gabrielson
  (Stackpole)
Fishes in the Home, by Ida M. Mellen (Dodd Mead)
Northern Fishes, by Samuel Eddy and Thaddeus Surber
  (University of Minnesota)

FROGS AND SALAMANDERS

Book of Amphibians and Reptiles, The, by Michael Bevans
  (Garden City)
Frogs and Polliwogs, by Dorothy Childs Hogner (Crowell)
Frogs and Toads, by Herbert Zim (Morrow)
Handbook of Frogs and Toads, by Anna A. and Albert H.
  Wright (Comstock) Cornell Univ.
Handbook of Salamanders, by Sherman C. Bishop (Comstock)
  Cornell Univ.
Reptiles and Amphibians of the Northeastern States, by Roger
  Conant, Zoological Society of Philadelphia.

INSECTS

Fieldbook of Insects, by Frank E. Lutz (Putnam)
Insect Guide, by Ralph B. Swain (Doubleday)
Junior Book of Insects, by Edwin Way Teale (Dutton)

TURTLES

Turtles, by Wilfrid Bronson (Harcourt Brace)
Turtles of the United States and Canada, by Clifford H. Pope
  (Knopf)
*Turtles: The Turtles of the United States, Canada, and Baja,
  California*, by Archie Carr (Comstock) Cornell Univ.

WATER (AND OTHER) PETS

Book of Wild Pets, The, by Clifford B. Moore (Branford)
Care of Water Pets, The, by Gertrude Pels (Crowell)
Home-made Zoo, by Sylvia S. Greenberg and Edith L. Raskin
  (David McKay)
How to Make a Miniature Zoo, by Vinson Brown (Little Brown)

WATER PLANTS

Aquatic Plants of the United States, by W. C. Muenscher
  (Comstock) Cornell Univ.

Manual of Aquatic Plants, by Norman C. Fassett (Univ. of
  Wisconsin)

GENERAL

Book of Nature Hobbies, The, by Ted Petit (Didier)
Fieldbook of Nature Activities, The, by William Hillcourt
  (Putnam)
Fieldbook of Ponds and Streams, by Ann Morgan (Putnam)
Hammond's Guide to Nature Hobbies, by E. L. Jordan
  (C. S. Hammond)
In Ponds and Streams, by Margaret Waring Buck (Abingdon)
Life of Inland Waters, by James G. Needham and J. F. Lloyd
  (Comstock) Cornell Univ.
Nature Notebook, by Robert Candy (Houghton, Mifflin)

BULLETINS AND LEAFLETS

"Common Fresh-water Fishes of the New York City Region,"
  Audubon Nature Bulletins, Nat'l Audubon Soc., 1130 5th
  Ave., New York 28, N.Y.
"Feeding Aquarium and Terrarium Animals," Turtox Service
  Leaflets, Gen. Biological Supply House, 761-763 E. 69th
  Place, Chicago 37, Illinois.
"Food of Bullheads," Document 1037, 1928, U.S. Bureau of
  Fisheries, Sup't of Documents, Washington, D.C.
"Fresh-water Aquarium, The," Audubon Nature Bulletins,
  Nat'l Audubon Soc., 1130 5th Ave., New York 28, N.Y.
"Fresh Water Fish," Conservation Information Series, Nat'l
  Wildlife Federation, 232 Carroll Street, N.W., Washington
  12, D.C.
"Frogs and Toads," Audubon Nature Bulletins, Nat'l Audubon
  Soc., 1130 5th Ave., New York 28, N.Y.
"Goldfish: Their Care in Small Aquaria and Ponds," Circular
  6, 1931, U.S. Bureau of Fisheries, Sup't of Documents,
  Washington, D.C.
"Keeping Native Fishes in Aquaria," by M. Gordon, Cornell
  Rural School Leaflet, Cornell Univ., Ithaca N.Y.
"Marine Fish," Conservation Information Series, Nat'l Wild-
  life Federation, 232 Carroll St., N.W., Washington 12, D.C.
"Salamanders," Audubon Nature Bulletins, Nat'l Audubon
  Soc., 1130 5th Ave., New York 28, N.Y.
"Starting and Maintaining a Balanced Fresh-water Aquarium,"
  Turtox Service Leaflets, General Biological Supply House,
  761-763 E. 69th Pl., Chicago 37, Illinois.
"Turtles," Audubon Nature Bulletins, Nat'l Audubon Soc.,
  1130 5th Ave., New York 28, N.Y.

MAGAZINES

Aquarium, Innes Publishing Company, 12th Street at Cherry,
  Philadelphia 7, Pa.
Junior Natural History, American Museum of Natural History,
  New York City.
Natural History, American Museum of Natural History, New
  York City.